The Cherry Picker's Daughter

Second Edition: A Childhood Memoir

Kerry Reed-Gilbert

16pt

Copyright Page from the Original Book

Published by Deadly Dingo Books
Imprint of Wild Dingo Press
Melbourne, Australia
books@wilddingopress.com.au
www.wilddingopress.com.au

First edition published by Deadly Dingo Books 2019
Second edition published by Deadly Dingo Books 2020

Text copyright © Kerry Reed-Gilbert 2019

The moral right of the author has been asserted.

Except as permitted under the Australian Copyright Act 1968, no part of this book may be reproduced, stored in a retrieval system, or transmitted in any form or by any means, electronic, mechanical, photocopying, recording, or otherwise without prior permission of the copyright owners and the publisher of this book.

Designer: Debra Billson
Painting on cover by Mathew Merritt, 2020
Editor: Catherine Lewis
Printed in Australia.

Reed-Gilbert, Kerry, 1956-2019, author.
The Cherry Picker's Daughter / Kerry Reed-Gilbert.

 A catalogue record for this book is available from the National Library of Australia

TABLE OF CONTENTS

Note from the publisher	i
Praise for The Cherry Picker's Daughter	iii
About the author	vii
Author's Note	x
Foreword	xiii
Acknowledgements	xvi

Part One

1: A town called Condo	3
2: One big Mob	11
3: My Island home	21
4: When the river floods	26
5: Bunyips, spirits and animals	35
6: Kids will be kids, and jumping fences	44
7: This old house	48
8: The silo and the Welfare Man	57
9: Going home to the Island	64
10: 'Your mother's dead'	67
11: Living at the cemetery	72

Part Two

12: Back on the Island	83
13: Daddy's home	90
14: Happy Christmas	96
15: 1964: my Island home all gone	119
16: Too many tents, too much heartache	127
17: What's a State Ward?	130
18: Cherry-picking time	136
19: All the way to Grafton Jail	143
20: Behind the bars	146
21: Earning a quid	152
22: The school's racist	161
23: Decimal currency in Sydney	164
24: Back to the paddocks	171

25: Blue, the 'hero' dog	176
26: Christmas under the cherry tree	182
27: Leeton Show and the Mormons	189
28: Morisset Mental Hospital	197
29: We got grandparents	200
30: Koora: the little town on the railway track	204
31: Pay day and trains, and getting shot at	211
32: Anzac Day and Martin Luther King	217
33: Mother's Day and White Trash	226
34: A letter from the Queen	233
35: Hearing the stories of my mother	243
36: Nearly fifteen	249
37: A fight and a visitor	255
38: The cherry pickers and the Tent Embassy	261
39: My mother's grave and the Gilbert name	271
40: A daughter's love	276
41: Motorbikes and life	283
42: Writing in Ghent, New York	285

Note from the publisher

The day after we received the very last corrections and amendments to the manuscript from Aunty Kerry, she quietly passed away on her final journey to the Tjukurpa. Right up to the end, we received the warmest, most caring emails from her, just making sure everything was in order, that the manuscript was exactly as she wanted it, that the photos were all there and the captions finalised and correct, that the cover was exactly as she envisaged. She touched our hearts with her love, her humility, her talents and an extraordinary life dedicated to helping others in so many ways. We feel both humbled and honoured that she trusted us with the task of bringing this important and timely story into the light of day at a time when Aboriginal history is being redefined and rewritten by First Nations' storytellers. All Australians need to know the truth of the lived experiences of our First Nations' sisters and brothers since Europeans arrived, and the rich cultural heritage that has sustained them through the recent brutal history, and their ancestors and this precious continent for millennia.

To that end, Wild Dingo Press has founded a new imprint with Wakka Wakka Wulli Wulli writer, academic and songwoman, Tjanara Goreng Goreng. Deadly Dingo Books has been set up to publish, exclusively, the work of First Nations' writers. *The Cherry Picker's Daughter* is the foundation title to be released by this new imprint. While the author dedicated her book to her Mummy, we dedicate our Deadly Dingo Books to the author, Kerry Reed-Gilbert.

Praise for The Cherry Picker's Daughter

A wonderful yarn by an Aboriginal Elder about a bygone way of life.
—Melissa Lucashenko, award-winning Goorie author, 2019 Miles Franklin award winner

The opening of this memoir is grounded in an acute sense of place and belonging. Kerry tells the reader: 'Our families have been here for a long, long time, right from the very start'. This unbroken connection to place and people permeates the narrative as Kerry recalls a life of tremendous difficulty and stress, always with a sense of unflappability, courage, determination and humour. 'You gotta laugh!' is a mantra that appears throughout the work...

The Cherry-Picker's Daughter is the book that all Australia needs to read for its testimony to courage, determination and resilience; and for what it says about activism that takes place a long way from public venues

and media. As the statement at the front makes clear: *This book is dedicated to Mummy.* The life of Joyce Hutchings should signal a reassessment of the way Aboriginal activism has been viewed to date.
 —Jeanine Leane, Wiradjuri writer and academic

If you were touched by *Growing Up Aboriginal in Australia,* you'll treasure this book. The exquisite prose is simple, matter-of-fact yet intimate, like a child whispering secrets to a friend. Aunty Kerry, a Wiradjuri elder, an activist, poet and educator, sadly passed in July, adding poignancy. Everyone should read this, and ponder how we unjustly trap people within our judgements.
 —Robert O'Hearn, *Booktopia*

The Cherry Picker's Daughter: a childhood memoir brings alive a true story of a blended Koori family in New South Wales in the 1950s through the eyes of a young daughter, the author. A hardworking Koori family, 'river people', building bridges across rivers, love, towns, racism, truths and

intergenerational trauma. The family's survival shaped by seasonal fruit-picking and a constant fear of the 'the welfare's' power to remove the children.
—Charmaine Papertalk Green, poet, writer and artist

Thank you, Kerry, for sharing your story—so much pain and hurt, but such life-affirming strength and love too.
—Kate Grenville AO, award-winning author

Kids bounce into this world with such capacity for hope and love and attachment; how painful it was to read the ways this was betrayed by an Australia that I wish had known better. This memoir felt important in my hands, historical, vital—and joyful. It described a childhood I needed to know, and filled me with deepest admiration and respect. I cried many tears for Kerry Reed-Gilbert and was so grateful for her wonderful Mummy.
—Sofie Laguna, award-winning author

An unflinching memoir of courage and resilience in the face of overwhelming odds by a remarkable Wiradjuri woman, that speaks to her spirit and strength and to the love and courage of the woman who raised her. An important book for all Australians.

—Joy Rhoades, author

At its heart, [*The Cherry Picker's Daughter*] is primarily a story of mothers and daughters both present and absent. This is a story about the fearlessness of Indigenous women; a stirring ode to a woman who worked to the bone to care for her children and to protect them as best she could from a world that threatened, ostracised and abused them. To borrow from Melissa Lucashenko's foreword, 'the fighting spirit of senior Wiradjuri women is a mighty thing'.

—Georgia Brough, *ArtsHub*

About the author

A Wiradjuri woman from Central New South Wales, **Aunty Kerry Reed-Gilbert** performed and conducted writing workshops nationally and internationally. She was the inaugural Chairperson of the First Nations Australia Writers Network (FNAWN) 2012–2015 and 2017–2018 and continued as Patron until she passed away in 2019. In 2013 she co-edited a collection of works *By Close of Business*. She was a member of the ACT Us Mob Writing (UMW) group and was FNAWN co-editor for the *Ora Nui* Journal collaboration between First Nations Australia writers and Maori writers.

In 2015, Kerry was shortlisted for the Story Wine Prize. In 2016 and 2017 she compiled and edited editions of *A Pocketful of Leadership in the ACT 2016* and *A Pocketful of Leadership in First Nations Australia Communities*, a collection of First Nations' voices from across Australia. Kerry was a former member of the Aboriginal Studies Press Advisory Committee and her poetry and prose have been published in many journals and anthologies nationally and internationally, including in the Macquarie PEN Anthology of Australian Literature. Her works have been translated into a number of languages including French, Korean, Bengali and Dutch.

This book is dedicated to Mummy.

Author's Note

My name is Kerry Reed-Gilbert and I am an Aboriginal Elder of the Wiradjuri Nation. My journey in this lifetime has been one of growing up as the youngest of eight in a family that was blended sixty years before that term became fashionable. My family was a mixture of cousins, and mostly, we came in twos. We were raised by 'Mummy', my father's older sister, Joyce. Mummy always has been my mother my entire life and hers. I am Mummy's baby.

My mother, Goma, who was a white woman, was murdered by my father, Kevin Gilbert, in January 1957 and buried at Parkes in New South Wales. My Aboriginal father was given a life sentence for this crime which dramatically changed all our lives, and he served fourteen and a half years before his release. In Long Bay Jail, he was known as Number 16.

Kevin Gilbert was my biological father who I have referred to here as 'my father' or 'the Old Man'. The term

'Daddy' refers not to Kevin Gilbert but rather to Ned Hutchings, the husband of Mummy. Daddy and Mummy Hutchings raised me and my brother, Kevin, along with their other children, both biological as well as other family members. As motherless kids whose father was in jail, my brother Kevin and I were made State Wards (along with our siblings, Paddy and Lynnie, after their own father, my Uncle Athol, one of Mummy's older brothers, died).

The story of my life as an Aboriginal ward of the State and cherry picker takes place mostly in Condobolin and Koorawatha. There are also sections set in Sydney, as well as Orange and Leeton, the fruit-picking districts of central and southern New South Wales.

These are my memories of growing up Koori within an extended family in country New South Wales, through the good times and bad. I have done my best to remember accurately, but they are a personal recollection of my life and my family's times.

To Kevin, Lynnie and Paddy: this book is ours.

Aunty Kerry Reed-Gilbert

Wiradjuri Nation
Canberra
2019

Foreword

When Aunty Kerry asked me to help her with her memoir of growing up as a fringe-dweller and fruit picker in the 1950s, she didn't have to ask me twice. I retained very clear memories of sitting at Griffith University in Brisbane as a young student, soaking up the words of her father, Kevin Gilbert, in his classic, *Living Black*. And I vividly remembered where I was in 1988, driving in my car and hearing Uncle Kevin's lacerating words coming over the ABC radio, 'I am not your "Aboriginal problem". You—and your Bicentenary—are mine'.

The idea that I might contribute in a small way to the next generation of the Gilbert family writing was as welcome as it was unexpected. As we talked over a few months, it was quickly evident that it was the lives of the fruit-picking poor which was central to Aunty Kerry's story. I'd known Aunty Kerry in Canberra for years as a tireless advocate for Aboriginal people and Aboriginal writing. And, of course being older, I knew that she must have lived through the era of active assimilation of Aboriginal people. I was not quite prepared though, for what I read in her draft manuscript. This is Australia's hidden history brought to light, and it is sobering to read what one Black family went through in mid-twentieth-century New South Wales. If Menzies had any forgotten Australians, these were surely them.

As young children, Kerry and her siblings lived on 'the Island', literally building and rebuilding their own bridge across the flooded Lachlan River so they could reach the town and school. Her Mummy took the kids along with her, following the fruit-picking seasons because that was one of the few ways for the very poor to survive. Their reality was of growing up always in makeshift housing, and constantly frightened of the hated Welfare coming to take away the kids; kids who became State Wards after the murder of Kerry's mother. Once, living on the edge of the local cemetery, for want of drinking water. And the love and connection of the extended Koori family overriding all this dire poverty, always. Kerry writes about 'the picking' and about what it is to be a child whose unknown father is incarcerated, far away, for a mysterious crime. Would he ever be released, and would he come home when he was? And what about the whispered rumours she had heard—were they true?

Around the time we finished our first round of edits, Aunty Kerry told me that someone had accused her of being a 'privileged Black'.

'If only they knew, hey?' she laughed. I laughed, too, for I knew that this memoir of her extraordinary life would be on the record soon enough.

This book taught me many things. First and foremost, it taught me that the fighting spirit of senior Wiradjuri women is a mighty thing. It also showed me that quiet achievers can be hiding in the most amazing stories. I hope you enjoy this window into Koori life, and the Koori world. I feel honoured to have played a small part in its coming to fruition.

Melissa Lucashenko
Meanjin-Brisbane
2018

Acknowledgements

This book started many years ago and has taken a long time to get here, but along the way, I have walked many miles (kilometres) with many people. Here are just a few. I have to say thank you to my daughters Lesa and Melanie, my grandkids and family. To Anita Heiss, thank you, Tidda, for sharing the journey; you've been there since the very beginning when I pulled my writing out of the drawer. A special mention to Kate Grenville for providing her support and expertise in the early stages of *The Cherry Picker's Daughter.* I couldn't have done it without you and Anita. To Melissa Lucashenko, thank you for working on the manuscript with me: I appreciate your guidance and sistahood. People such as Cathy Craigie, Jeanine Leane, Yvette Holt, Charmaine Green, Sharon Mununggurr, Barbara Nicholson, Jared Thomas: I treasure each step we took together. Special mention has to be for Geoff Ross and Tony Duke: thank you both for everything.

It's important that I remember to acknowledge the Us Mob Writers (UMW) group and especially Samantha Faulkner and Lisa Fuller: thanks for our KLaS meetings, loved every one of them. Just as important is the First Nations Australia Writers Network (FNAWN): here's to all the deadlies from Jimmy Everett and the working party, to all Board members past and present and our FNAWNees: thanks for making my life special.

Many thanks to Cathi, Alex and Jessica from Wild Dingo Press. Thanks for taking a chance on *The Cherry Picker's Daughter.* I hope you're as proud of it as me.

Last but not least is you, the reader. Thank you for picking my book up and taking it home—it's a story to be shared.

In Unity,
Aunty Kerry Reed-Gilbert

Part One

1

A town called Condo

Family reunion, here at last! It's taken many years to make ours happen, we're a big Mob. A big Wiradjuri family scattered from pillar to post across this land. It's happening on the Island, my Island home. We've had many happy years living here; it was a place where I lived when I was young. Throughout the years, the mere mention of Condo and the Island brings wonderful memories, touched with a tinge of 'if only'.

Sparks crackle from the fire burning. Meat is sizzling, sausage sandwiches are happening with kids running around, making it one of the happiest days of my life. We're back in a place where memories flash before your eyes and tears and laughter hit you at the same time. This spot is where our house used to be before it got burnt down many years ago; suddenly a wave of sadness hits me. The night creeps in as the kids get put to bed in one of the many tents pitched around the yard. The men pull up empty drums and chairs for us women so we can sit around the fire. My grandsons find *the best chair in the house* for me they reckon, all the while telling me to watch out for the shaky leg and not to wiggle around in my seat too much.

'Haha,' I tell them, 'it's hard to stop these old bones from creaking, let alone wiggle anymore'.

Pricking my ears is the voice of my brother Paddy, he's the best storyteller. He can tell them big ones as well; whether they're true or not, I love listening to his yarns. No matter what, you know *it's gonna be a beauty.* Big booms of laughter thump my ears as tears roll down my face, pains start way down in my belly hurting from too much laughter.

Slowly a piercing pain sears my heart through the laughter as the emptiness rears its ugly head and I gulp back the tears of missing her. Glancing around the fire, I watch people and their shadows. A smile counters my sadness as I listen to others who, just like me, still roll their R's and can't pronounce their H's as they speak. Hidden within the faces of the oldies, a glimpse of grief flickers and I know they, too, are missing loved ones who have gone to our Ancestors. Tears gush and this time it's not from laughter. I say a little prayer to Mummy, telling her how much I love her and that we shall be together again soon.

Flames are dancing high as the heat penetrates my ageing body. I slip back into my memories as the two of us walk up the main street of Condobolin, Condo for short. Sitting in the centre of New South Wales, a hot dusty old town kissed by the bank of the Lachlan River. It's 1960. I'm four, all dressed up in my town clothes, and I'm real proud because I'm with Mummy and she loves me and that's the most important thing in the world.

We've just walked up from down the bottom end of the main street over a little dirt road, through the gutters and onto the best place in the world: our little piece of paradise—the Island, that's where we live. The gutters lead us up to the tar and cement of Bathurst Street and back again. A little dirt road called Baxter Street takes us through the gutters then home to the Island. The gutters—that's what we call the dry riverbed that divides our home from the streets of Condo. It's not really an island but everyone calls it that.

'Where we going today, Mummy?'

'Up the street.'

'What we gonna do, Mummy?' my child's voice asks.

'We gonna say hello to Scotty and maybe go somewhere special.'

'Where Mummy, where's special?' I'm hoping we go to the Red Rose Café for a milkshake and an ice cream.

Feeling real lucky today, the sun beams down on us both. It's only Mummy and me because all the other kids are at school. People will see me holding her hand. Today I'm walking on clouds. I look like a fairy all dressed up pretty in pink. My dress swirls around when I spin and my black shoes are bright and shiny and my white socks are frilly. Today I have my town clothes on. What a magical day it is.

Glancing up at Mummy, she is dressed up, too, a black handbag swings over her arm. There's not a hair out of place and she looks so beautiful; she's wearing her town clothes, too. We have clothes that we wear at different times: house clothes, town clothes and cherry-picking clothes (they're our real old clothes). We have show clothes, too, for when the show comes to town in August but today, I got to dress up in the prettiest clothes ever.

Happiness is my world; I want everyone to see us. Scotty at the post office comments on how pretty I look. I glow. He tells Mummy to have a good day as we walk out the door into the sun; the heat smacks you in the face like a hard pillow. I'm sweating already but nothing can bother me today. Today I'm the happiest girl in the whole wide world.

People in town all say hello to us, both Blackfellas and Whitefellas, too. My Mummy is well-respected in the town. Even the policeman, the old sergeant, likes Mummy. He always calls her Mrs Hutchings, real respectful like. One time, Darryl was in real trouble and he came and told her about it first; I think he had to leave town 'in a hurry'. Our families have been here for a long, long time, right from the very start. Back in the early days, all the Aboriginal families used to live on the Murie, four kilometres along the road going south. My Old Granny Murray and all the other Blackfellas lived there.

After seeing Scotty at the post office, we go and say hello to the lady in Fossey's and Mummy has a good talk to her while I look at all the dolls. Pulling me away from the toys, she says it's time to go. Walking down the street, we head to the Red Rose Café; a chocolate milkshake is waiting just for me. If we would have went the other way, we would have ended at the fish-and-chip shop owned by Uncle Archie and Aunty Isabel; they're Daddy's family and too far to walk today. Soon it's time to go and I hold her hand as we walk, happy to be going home to where I belong.

Mummy is really my Aunty Joyce—my father Kevin's sister and she is married to Daddy who is really my Uncle Ned. Us younger kids don't know this. We only know that we are Mummy and Daddy's. Daddy's not around much since he works away on the railway a real lot—he's a fettler. He comes visiting when he's not working. He rides one of those funny trolley cars that go up and down. Daddy stands on one end and another man on the other and they pump away 'up and down, up and they go'.

Mummy looks after us kids and she gets work wherever she can, stick-picking, felling trees (she can swing an axe better than a man), cooking at the pub or cleaning houses. Mummy's cleaning houses around this time when I'm four. I don't go to school yet, so I go to work with her. The lady's house she cleans is real big and lovely—made of red bricks and has real old stuff inside. It's got all these things in it that I've never seen before and I might break something! Standing in a corner, there's a china cabinet full of little ornaments. We have ornaments, too, but not like these. I'm not allowed to go inside by myself. The stuff is real pretty but I play outside in the sun with the family's cat near the back step.

Smoko time and Mummy gives me drinks and biscuits and I share them with the cat. She gobbles them up real fast, then she wants the rest of mine. I call her a guts. I also play with my marbles, making a little circle in the dirt. I carry them everywhere in my pocket, along with my hanky. I wish Kevin, my brother, was here so we could play together but he's a year older than me and is at school. I play outside until Mummy tells me it's time to go home. She tells me I'm a good girl, and then we start walking home. I'm happy, but after cleaning that big house, Mummy's exhausted.

We head back to the Island where we belong.

2

One big Mob

A big Mob we are; my family is pretty big. There's a real lot of us and I know who they all are. Or I think I do.

There's lots of us kids. Eight all up and we are sort of divided into two lots of four. Three of us are Mummy and Daddy's biological kids, and five of us aren't. There's Johnny, Meryl and Maureen and Darryl: they are the four big ones in my family. Johnny, Meryl and Maureen are Mummy's and Daddy's. Darryl isn't Mummy's biological son. He belongs to Aunty Flora and so he's really our cousin like the others, but he's regarded as a brother just like the other brothers.

Then us four younger ones: Paddy, Lynnie, Kevin and me. I'm the baby. Lynnie and Paddy's real father is Mummy's older brother, Uncle Athol. Uncle Athol was a top boxer in the Riverina; he used to fight in the shows that travelled round. Lynnie and Paddy are real proud of him; we all are.

When they were just babies, Uncle Athol died in a car accident in Shepparton. Before he died, he had always said that, if anything happened to him, that Mummy had to take his kids and keep them. That's why Mummy took them on to raise up as her own, like Kevin and me.

'What about me and Kevin?' I ask, curious.

Lynnie tells me that our real mother died and that our real father is Kevin, Mummy's younger brother. I think it's strange how Lynnie and Paddy's real father died and me and Kevin's real mother died, and we all end up belonging to Mummy. All my family are different colours—white, brown and black. We know we're Aboriginal and we also know we're not like other families. Lynnie tells me that's why the Welfare comes and I know I don't like the Welfare.

Lynnie won't tell me no more after that. She says not to tell anyone she told; she'll get a hiding and we all hate that. If I tell, she'll give me a hiding herself. Lynnie tells me more about the Welfare though.

'He's the white man in the big suit that comes here sometimes. The man who can take us away from Mummy if he wants to,' she tells me. 'He don't need a reason. We're Aboriginal so we always have to be good and give him no reason to take us away.'

As I get older and I hear the threat of the Welfare over and over, fear grabs my heart each time anybody mentions his name. I ask Lynnie where me and Kevin's father is but she won't tell me. She tells me not to worry. She says to make sure I don't mention my father in front of anyone, especially Mummy as she'll get upset.

I don't ask any questions. Deep down in my heart, I don't want to know. I'm dreading the answers. I know without it being spoken that some things about me and Kevin and Lynnie and Paddy make us different.

Some people do bad things to us kids but we can't say anything to Mummy. They said they'll tell Joyce that we were bad so she wouldn't want us anymore because we're 'naughty'; and they'll let the Welfare know that we were 'bad kids and he would take you away'. Tears are streaming down my face as my sister wraps her arms around me as I promise I'll be a real good girl and won't say a word so no one can take us from Mummy.

I'm frightened about this talk of being different and the Welfare, but ultimately, I don't care. I've got Mummy, a woman who loves us and who works real hard making sure we've got plenty to eat, clean clothes and a roof over our heads. She makes sure that we're clean and tidy and safe. I don't want no other mother or father. This Mummy and Daddy, my brothers and sisters, we all seem to fit together. I'm the baby of them all, I'm Dolly. My sister Maureen calls me that. She said, 'when you were a baby, you had the biggest brown eyes and looked just like a baby doll'.

We sometimes do things together as a family but, mainly, it's us four younger ones and Mummy. Some of the bigger ones are grown up and don't live with us anymore. On our Island, us younger ones play and laugh together and have a good time. We visit our relations on the Mission and in town. We don't go to white people's houses, only to our own family. The only white houses we ever go to are the ones Mummy cleans.

Aunty Tilly, Aunty Dolly and Aunty Rosie, Uncle Paddy and Uncle Teddy, our Great Uncles and Aunties, they're real special people and they can speak Aboriginal language. All them old ones, they're all our Granny's brothers and sisters. Granny's name was Rachel Naden before she married our grandfather, John Gilbert, but Granny and Grandfather both died when Mummy was young so we are left now with Great Uncles and Aunties instead.

We love it when our Old Uncles come to visit. We're allowed to say hello and then we go outside to play so they can have a good yarn. The Old Uncles go rabbiting and they hang all the dead rabbits on the pushbike. I reckon one day there was a hundred hanging there. They sell them so they can earn a quid but they always give Mummy some to feed us kids.

Uncle Paddy and Aunty Carol and all their kids, Little Lynnie, Rocky, Willie, Rachel and Johnny all come visit as well. They live in Condo, too. One day, my Aunty Flora came, that's Mummy's baby sister who is Darryl's real mother. She came with all her other kids, another Lynnie, Aileen and Smokey (that's his nickname). They had a funny-looking car that looked like a T-model Ford and we all got to have a ride in it. It was a beauty!

***

My biggest sister, Meryl, comes home for a visit. She's getting grown up now. She comes back from the Aboriginal Bible College in Singleton and she's in love with Slugga. He's nice. Slugga and his family live on the Mission across the riverbank from us. He brings his guitar and sings to her.

In the afternoon, when the sun's going down, Slugga always comes over and serenades her. They sit on the hard ground together and the wind starts blowing the dirt all around us. Meryl knows I love music and she calls me over. Leaning the guitar on his knee, he starts to sing 'Roses are red, my love'.

I beam, happy; he says I'm as pretty as my big sister. Meryl reckons good looks run in our family and Mummy's real pretty, too. Happiness for me—I take after my big sister! It's a beautiful day. The sun is smiling real bright, just like me.

Sister Maureen loves a fella called Sam; she loves him so bad all she does is talk about him. She's been in love with him since she was a little girl. When he comes, me and Lynnie look at each other, not saying a word. We don't want to be there when he's around so we head to the paddock saying, 'We seen a spiny anteater and we gotta find it'. We don't talk to each other about him; we don't like him being near us but we can't say a word to anyone. The threat of the Welfare!

We get other visitors, too. Monty, he's like Mummy's big brother; he comes and cuts the big wood for her and she gives him a feed. We like Monty. Me and Lynnie play a game; when we see him coming, we run and hide and he's gotta find us. Only our family and other Aboriginal people visit our house—never Whitefellas, except the Welfare.

A big Mob we are and we got a lot of Paddys and Lynnies in our family. There's Little Paddy, my brother, Uncle Paddy, Mummy's brother, and our Old Great Uncle Paddy. And we got lotsa Lynnies, too. Big Lynnie, my sister, Little Lynnie, Uncle Paddy's daughter, and Lynnie, Aunty Flora's daughter, who is Darryl's real sister. Lynnie, she's bigger and older than Big Lynnie and Little Lynnie but she lives a long way away. Aunty Flora took them all to Western Australia to live, a long time ago.

All us kids are different, too. Darryl, he's the same age as Maureen but they got different birthdays, hers in June and his in April. Him and Maureen say they are twins. They are ten years older than me. Darryl calls Mummy 'Aunty Joyce' and he's not like us other kids.

'How come he don't call Mummy, Mummy,' I ask Lynnie.

She tells me, 'Darryl's Aunty Flora's boy but Mummy's rearing him up'.

She asks me if I remember Aunty Flora and her family visiting in a big old car. I tell her, yes. Mummy has a photo of her with the car and all us kids on it. Mummy and her photos—she's real fussy about them and always makes sure we're real careful when we look at them. She loves to take the photos out and tell you all about our family. Mummy says if we ever in trouble, we have to look to the Black side of our family, never the white side. That's the Gilbert side, her father's family.

Our mob, it's big and it's wonderful and the best time is when we all come together and have barbecues down on the riverbank. It's just round the bend from the Bunyip's hole. On Boxing Day, we all gather down there every year and we celebrate all the family coming together. The Boxing Day barbecue is for the ones who couldn't make it home on Christmas Day.

I'm happy with my family; we really are the best. I love my sisters and brothers (even if they tease me) and I love Mummy and Daddy, too. When our cousins come to visit, there's a lot of us and we play out on the road. We have lots of fun playing pick-up sticks, hide'n-go-seek and "Simon says". We play for hours until it gets dark or it's time to do our jobs.

We do lots of other good things with our family, too. We go rabbiting or duck-hunting with Uncle Paddy, Mummy's brother. I love duck-hunting. All us kids swim into the river to catch the ducks. We all dive in the water and try to sneak up on them. We try to catch as many as we can. Us kids have a race to see who can get the most.

We go rabbiting, too, and we always have a good feed later but Uncle Paddy sells the best ones. He reckons, 'You gotta earn a quid the best way you can and get a good feed to boot'.

3

My Island home

The Island. It sounds special and it is. Our Island is our playground and our world. We share it with two other families. There's only three houses and they're all spread out. There's a big old rambling house in the middle of the street, that's where we live. Our house fits us all, even when the big ones are visiting. Plenty of room to move. Us kids and May's kids (next door), we play games out the front on the road. May Smith and all her kids' house is closer to the gutters and there's another house way past us down the bottom the other way. When Maureen marries Sam, she lives in that house, too.

No tar and cement here, not like what they have up in town. The dirt is smooth as silk but, when the sun is beating down it burns our feet and gets in between your toes. Screams of 'Ooh, ooh, ooh' spill out of our mouths on really hot days. One day, Mummy ran out the door thinking something was wrong; then she saw all us kids hopping on our tiptoes from the scalding ground as we tried to get to the shade of the tree. Busting out laughing, she said we looked funny tiptoeing; then we all started cackling, too. Feeling sorry for us with our burning feet, she brings us a drink as we sit under our favourite tree.

It's also Cocky's favourite tree. A loud squark booms its way through the air. We look up and Cocky's screaming, stirring up a storm, screaming out to Mummy. He's a Major Mitchell; they're a type of native cockatoo named after that old explorer that came here.

The gutters separate us from the town. We call it the gutters but it's really the riverbed that holds the river when it's full. It's dried out most of the time. It's made up of dirt and rocks—a huge bus could park in there, I reckon. There are lots of gum trees and lots of native hop bushes that line the riverbank, guarding us from the town and from strangers.

On the far side of the Island, the river flows all year long. That's where we go swimming and where we cart our water from, too. All the water we need for drinking or cooking or anything, we bring it up from the river. Nearly every day, we have to carry our water up to the house. When Maureen lives in the house down that way, fingers are crossed that she'll see us and come say hello.

The Mission is down past there, too, on the other side of the river. The Lachlan River flows between us. The Mission is where a lot of our families now live, as well as in town and on Boona Road; we go and visit family at these places all the time. Between us and the Mission, we have a little footbridge that gets people from that side to ours. This way they don't have to walk so far to town.

When the river comes up and floods, we need a boat to get off the Island but we haven't got a boat so that means we have to leave. When that happens, we have to go and live in a tent somewhere around town. One time, during a flood, we stayed on the Island as long as we could, avoiding school. Afterwards, Lynnie said the Welfare said to Mummy, 'The kids gotta go to school'. The fear of the Welfare! When the river goes down, then we come home again. Living in the tent is good but we make sure that we have clean drinking water close by.

The Island is the best place in the world to live. The river is our playground. We have a couple of swimming spots. Paddy, he's the best swimmer, he can go under the water for the longest time. Mummy took us to the pictures one day and we saw *Tarzan.* Paddy can swim just like him, so when we're swimming, we call him Tarzan. I'm sure he shows off just a little bit more when we call him that.

We have our two dogs, Poidy and Rex. They're our protectors. We're not allowed to go down to the river unless they go with us. Mummy tells them dogs to 'look after us'. I'm sure they know they would get into a lot of trouble if something happened to one of us kids on their watch. Their faces look straight at her as she speaks—I reckon they know what she's saying. They look at her and then us.

Laughing and happy, we run and get our swimmers on and grab a towel each and head down to our favourite spot. Rex stands on the riverbank barking at us, wanting us to get outta the water and go home. We play games with them. When we're swimming, Poidy thinks we're drowning and tries to save us all the time. We tease him, sing out to him. He swims out to one of us, then we'll dive under the water.

While he searches for us slowly, we come up for air and let him grab our arm in his mouth to pull us up; we tell him he's 'a good boy'. Paddy can hold his breath the longest and he keeps ducking under the water making Poidy try to find him. Lynnie, Kevin and me laugh as Poidy paddles around in circles until he spots Paddy, his favourite, and then he pulls him up.

Our dogs don't like no one smacking us either. Poidy and Rex don't mind Mummy going crook on us but they don't like anyone else doing it. Mummy don't like anyone going crook on us, either, so the big boys only give us a hard time when she's not home. Especially Paddy and Kevin—they give the boys, especially Paddy, a harder time than us girls.

4

When the river floods

The river's flowing! We all love living on the Island. Sometimes, when we get flooded, we gotta make a rock bridge so we can go to town or school. When the water starts to rise, we need to carry rocks; the more it rises, the more we carry. It takes a long time to build the bridge, even when all of us are doing it.

Paddy, Lynnie and Mummy carry the bigger ones. Stacking the rocks on top of each other our bridge starts to take shape. Me and Kevin's job is to fill up the gaps with the smaller rocks. We race to see who can fill the holes up the best. Making the bridge, searching for big and little rocks, is such fun.

Hearing a groan, we look over and see Mummy struggling to lift a great big rock—her legs are buckling. The boys run to help; they each grab a part of that rock and help hold it in her arms, taking dolly steps as they walk together till the rock is in place.

Every now and again, we all try to carry the real big rocks so that we can help more but Mummy tells us not to as we could hurt ourselves. It's taken several days but, finally, the bridge is all done and Mummy walks across a few times to make sure that it's safe. Standing on different stones, legs firmly placed rocking side to side, she makes sure that no rock is loose so none of us can slip off as we walk across.

Soon the river's rising fast and the water is flowing between the rocks. We wait now for the floodwater to hit us. It doesn't take long before we put our bridge to the test. So far, we can walk across with our shoes on—the bridge is still higher than the water. Mummy reckons, 'In a couple of days, we're gonna have to build it up more'. And we do!

One day, Paddy runs down to the gutters before us and then he runs back saying the river has risen. The water's starting to come over the bridge and we have to take our shoes and socks off so they don't get wet. Mummy walks the bridge, testing it as she goes. Lynnie carries my shoes, just in case I slip and lose them. If I did, I'd never see them again.

Walking in front of me, Lynnie tells me I gotta put my feet on the same rock, in the same spot as she does. Feeling like I'm splitting in half, I stretch my legs out real wide. I'm stretching till I can't stretch no more and it hurts. Sometimes I wonder if I'm gonna split in half. Making it to the other side of the riverbank, I tell my big sister that I was walking in her footsteps. We both giggle.

Watching Paddy and Kevin begin their dangerous journey to reach us, we hold our breath. Kevin's placing his feet where Paddy did. He's stretching as far as he can go. I wonder if Kevin ever worries about being split in half, too. We're all happy when we're on the other side together.

The kids go to school and I go with Mummy. After school, the other kids run home yelling out to Mummy, telling her that the water's coming up fast and we won't be able to walk on our bridge tomorrow.

The next morning, we head down to the gutters and the water has risen higher and the current is strong. Our bridge of rocks and stones has been carried away by this force of nature. We don't even try to walk over the bridge anymore. It's a long way to the other side. The river current is strong—it's already taken some of my cousins away, making them drown, even though they were all grown up.

The kids still have to go to school, though, and since Mummy won't let me try to walk in the water by myself now, she's gonna have to piggyback me. There's a big old gum tree standing beside the riverbank and I climb up onto the branches to get onto her shoulders so she can carry me across.

Reaching up, Lynnie passes me up a big bundle of our clothes that I need to carry while I'm way up high on Mummy's shoulders. I grab it and hold it close to my chest. I'm a little bit scared as I can't really hold on but I reach down and grab a piece of her shirt and, with the other one hand, I clench real tight around the bundle. What a balancing act!

Stepping into the river real slow, Mummy takes nerve-racking steps, testing the water and the bottom of the river. She's got goose bumps all over her arms so the water must be real cold. She takes a few steps and the water's halfway up to her knees already. The current is fighting her body, trying to push us down the river. I feel her body stiffen; I hold my breath. The water's creeping higher and higher. Mummy's wet over her knees now. I watch the water swirl around her body. She's trying to hold my legs out so they don't get wet.

I'm sitting on Mummy's shoulders, finally bigger than the other kids. I twist my head around to look at them, smiling, forgetting about the danger and happy to be where I am at this moment. Mummy tells me to sit still; she holds my legs tighter, just below the knees. I can tell in her voice that she's getting cranky with me for squirming around. I turn around real quick.

The river, it's got a mind of its own. It's trying to push Mummy and me downstream. Her body is tense and strong as she grips my legs tighter, fighting the current with all her might. She's careful with each step she takes, testing where her foot is gonna go as she walks.

It's one step at a time and we need to be careful; she might trip on one of those rocks and lose her balance. If she falls, we'll both end up floating down the Lachlan River, for sure. I'm way up high, holding my breath and praying that there's not a great big rock, waiting for her to step and trip.

She takes me over to the town side and goes back after the others. She brings Kevin first—he's gotta hold the belt on the back of her dress and not let go, and so do the others. My heart is beating real quick, watching every step they make. I sit watching, praying for them all to get through the water safe. We all can swim but we know that none of us is good enough to beat the flooded river. I'm happy when Mummy, my sister and two brothers are all standing beside me.

Us girls get dressed first, behind the bushes. The boys are shivering with a towel wrapped around their wet bodies, yelling at us to hurry up so they can get out of their wet clothes, too. They play cockatoo (lookout) up the top of the gutters, with their backs turned away from us. They let us know if anyone is coming so they sing out real loud 'cooeeeeeee' and then us girls do the same for them. We all play cockatoo for Mummy but she always waits until we're dressed before she changes.

We hang our wet clothes over the trees and bushes to dry out for when we come home. The riverbank looks real funny with towels and wet clothes thrown all over the place. We know all our clothes will be there when we return.

***

Soon enough, a day or two later, the river is raging. The kids can't go to school no more and Mummy can't work. We ain't got no boat so we're stuck on the Island but us kids are happy. Pawsy, our neighbour from across the river, they got one. They own the paddock beside us with the big fig tree on it. We're not allowed to go onto their land but we love raiding his fruit trees.

Mummy doesn't like to ask to borrow their boat unless it's an emergency. We don't ask people for nothing. We don't do nothing that has attention drawn to us. We gotta be dressed well, have ironed clothes, bobby pins in the hair, always have shoes on in town and a spotless house. Everything we do is about avoiding the attention of the white people and, ultimately, the Welfare, at all costs. It's not safe to ask white people for anything. All the Aboriginal people in Condo know this. People's houses, tents and tin shacks were spotless, for fear of kids being stolen away.

One day, Kevin's sick, real sick, and the river's too high to cross. He has to go to the doctor. Mummy tells brother Paddy to go and wait down the riverbank till he sees Mr Pawsy or his son feeding his cows on the other side. He's to yell out and tell him Kevin's sick, and ask him if we can borrow the boat, please? Mr Pawsy gets his son to bring it over. Paddy rows the boat for Mummy to take Kevin to the hospital.

He stays in hospital and then Mummy comes home. Mummy offers to pay for the use of the boat but Mr Pawsy wouldn't take anything—he's a good man. We borrow the boat when Kevin comes home.

    A proud woman, Mummy is. She takes nothing for nothing.

5
Bunyips, spirits and animals

Dusk on the Island is beautiful. Us kids play out in the red dirt that makes up our road. It's there we play together and with the kids next door and our cousins. Another visitor lives with us on the Island, too, just over the road. There's a bush with a spirit in it. Every night he comes out and watches us at play. We wait, watching for him to move but he don't. He just stays there, stuck in that bush, never stirring. He hides in the bush thinking we can't see him but his whiteness shines through the branches. We know it's a spirit. We try to chase him away but he won't go.

We even throw stones at him but still he stays right there. As each stone sails past, our throats are in our mouths. Each time a stone flies, we all stand crouched ready to run just in case, by some miracle, he gets hit and decides he's gonna come and get us. I reckon we all miss him, deliberately, and are really scared of him, too.

In the morning, we run outside to see if he's still there but he's gone. He only comes at dusk. We know he'll be there as the sun goes to sleep for another day. Soon, we stop trying to scare him away and leave him alone. I reckon he must wanna live on the Island, too.

And we got other spirits, too, down at the riverbank near the bridge that takes us over to the Mission side of the river. Sometimes, you can hear people crying and yelling out.

Lynnie says, 'That's the spirits of the people who drowned in the river'.

Tears well in my eyes as she says, 'They're crying. They wanna go home and they can't get to the other side.'

I ask her, 'What's the other side?' She tells me to go to sleep. Sometimes, I lie in bed at night and I can hear a baby cry, and I close my eyes real tight and try not to hear.

Lots of animals live with us on the Island. It's like a big menagerie. Cocky, he sits up in the tree all day and watches me and Kevin play our favourite game, marbles. We reckon he's our babysitter, looking after us for Mummy. When the other kids aren't around, Cocky makes sure we don't do nothing wrong. I'm sure he's evil, though. When no one's looking, he flies at me, flapping his wings and squawking. I run from him, screaming. He never catches me or hurts me, just scares me. He doesn't pick on Kevin or Paddy or Lynnie, only me.

But when I'm chucking a real tantrum, Mummy says to him, 'Get her, Cocky'. He chases me all over the yard, trying real hard to catch me. I don't like him much when he does this but it works. I stop my tantrum.

Cocky, he's a real troublemaker, too. He sits in the tree and gets up to lotsa mischief. Like Poidy and Rex, he knows we're not allowed to go to the river by ourselves. He watches Paddy like a hawk, too. If he can't see Paddy, he screams out to Mummy, 'Paddy's down the river!'

Mummy always comes out and asks Cocky, 'where's Paddy?' and he tells her, 'Paddy's down the river,' even if he's not.

She tells him that 'Paddy's at school' and Cocky's happy, and then, finally, he decides to go to sleep. Cocky, he keeps me on my toes all the time. He's worse than a watchdog. He's special and he loves us kids but he brings me such heartache.

We've got two magpies called Heckle and Jeckle who play with us when we play marbles. One day, Jeckle's leg is missing and Kevin said I did it. But I know I never would do anything like that. I stamp my feet, chucking a tantrum, and still they wouldn't believe me. I reckon he musta got it caught in some wire, otherwise I reckon Kevin was the one who cut off his leg, only pretending it was me. Not me—I don't like blood.

As well as Cocky and the dogs and the magpies, we also have Bertha, our pig. She's big, fat and spoilt. She loves us all, too, and follows us everywhere. This one year, she had eighteen babies. She followed sister Maureen up Bathurst Street one day with all her babies following behind her. The man from the newspaper took their photo and put it in the paper the next day. Mummy put the photo in the family collection, but when our house got burnt down, the photo got destroyed. We had a goat and we used to milk her and drink her milk, too.

We got chooks and a rooster as well, and the rooster is real mean. When I have to go outside to use the toilet, he chases me madly, flapping his wings. The toilet, it's one of them old ones that has a hole dug in the dirt and some corrugated tin wrapped around it and a hessian bag as a door. I can't go out the back by myself. The rooster always chases me but he's not like Cocky who never catches me. The rooster, when he catches me, he bites me on the bum and it hurts. When he does that, I just stand and scream and scream. I scream out at the top of my lungs for someone to come and save me.

Big tears run down my face as I tell the rooster I hate him and I don't want him to live on the Island with us anymore. I would be so happy if he went away for good. Tears are rolling down my cheeks and I gulp to catch my breath as I ask Mummy, 'Why can't the rooster live somewhere else?'

She looks at me and laughs, telling me 'not to be silly'.

There's a Bunyip down the river, too. Us kids, we go down there and try to see him but we're real careful—we don't wanna make him mad at us. He's under a big old willow tree that guards his sacred spot. One time, we climb out on a fat old log that sticks up outta the water. I climb out real careful, testing the log first so I make sure I don't slip, then I stretch my body way out over the water.

Paddy and Kevin are on the riverbank and Lynnie and me are crowded on the log together. I get scared she'll rock the log and shake me off. We're hanging onto the branches and I hold on for dear life, and she points his hole out to me. I look but all I can see is pretty colours swirling down in the water. His waterhole is made up of all the colours of the rainbow that are swishing about.

I gaze at the colours, I look real hard but I can't see him at all. I tell them 'I can see him', pretending, so they don't think I'm stupid and blind. I'm still looking, straining my eyes searching, but Lynnie has sneaked back onto the riverbank and left me out there all alone.

A plop thuds in my ears as one of the boys chucks a stone right near me. They scream at me, 'He's coming to get you, Kerry'. They start running away. I scream. I let go of the willow branches and try to jump from the log onto the bank. I miss and my feet go into the mud. I slip further down! Panic grips me as I try desperately to grab the grass on the dry part of the riverbank.

I nearly fall backwards into the Bunyip's hole! Scrambling, I pull myself out of the water and I start running. I run fast, screaming and trying to catch my breath at the same time. I don't stop until I get back to the house and I have a stitch in my side, and it hurts.

They're laughing at me. They tricked me; he wasn't coming at all. I start yelling. I look down at my feet and they're all covered in mud. I wash my feet with water from the bucket before Mummy sees me. We're not allowed to go down to the Bunyip's hole and I'd be in real trouble if she knows. They're still teasing me. I threaten to dob them in to Mummy so they finally leave me alone. It's hard being the youngest sometimes.

It's not just spirits and bunyips and pets. Snakes live on the Island, too. Sometimes, if the water's rising, when we cart our water up to the house, dozens of snakes will be swimming from the Mission side of the riverbank to our side.

I ask Mummy, 'Why?' She tells me, 'They're trying to get away from the rising water'. She says, 'You're not to go down there; don't go near there'. I quickly promise not to. There's no way I'm going near them.

Those snakes must love our place, too—they come crawling all over our yard during summer. When Mummy finds one, she gets the shovel and breaking its back kills it dead. Snake bites can kill so we have to be real careful of snakes. They might bite one of us and their poison can make us real sick or we can even die.

One day, when I was about six, I picked up this old piece of tin and there was a lot of baby snakes under it, wriggling around. Paddy and Kevin got some sticks and started playing with them until Mummy came and saw what they were doing. She went crook and then she killed the snakes, hitting them with the back of the shovel.

When she kills the big snakes, she hangs them over the wire fence past Cocky's tree. Sometimes, she kills more than one a day. I think Mummy's trying to tell the other snakes not to come and live in our backyard. They're dead if they do. One day, when I came home from school, there was about a dozen just hanging over our fence, dead as can be. I tried to count them but there were too many. Mummy doesn't have to worry about me playing with snakes. If I see one, I will just scream out to her at the top of my lungs, 'Snake, Mummy!' and she'll come running with her shovel. It's just one more way she looks after us and protects us from any kind of harm.

6

Kids will be kids, and jumping fences

One day, sister Lynnie was climbing on the bookcase when it fell on her. There was a scream and a big crash; she was knocked out and had to go to bed. Me and the two boys had to keep checking on her while Mummy finished off all her jobs.

We sneaked up to the bed and listened to see if we can hear her breathing. The boys reckon, 'Lynnie's not breathing. She's dead.' I don't believe them and say they're lying but Kevin reckons he can prove it. He goes and gets the lid of the Sunshine milk tin and holds it up close to her mouth. He tells me, 'If there's no fog, then there's no breath coming out and that means she's dead'.

He holds the lid close and I watch, eyes glued, for that fog to appear. I wanna know my sister is alive and just asleep; I don't want her to be dead.

Kevin pulls the lid away from her mouth and there's nothing, no fog; nothing, not one sign to say my sister is alive. I'm about to cry when Paddy tells Kevin to do it again. He does and still there's no fog on the lid. Tears start rolling down my face and I turn to run screaming to Mummy but Paddy catches me before I make it out the door, putting his hand over my mouth, telling me to quieten down. I stand, tears running like a tap as I watch my sister laying on that bed, not moving one inch, not one breath of air coming out of her lungs.

The boys reckon they can bring her back to life. I'm stuck watching her body, wondering what would happen next. Her eyelids flicker. I hold my breath, wishing she would be alright. All of a sudden, Lynnie opens her eyes and starts laughing. The boys join in; they got me again! I walk outta the room, threatening to tell. Their laughter echoes behind me. Us four younger ones get on pretty good except when they tease me, and then we fight.

There are lotsa trees and bushes scattered all around the Island. There's even some big old fig trees and quince trees down the back in Pawsy's paddocks. When they're ripe, we sneak down and pick a heap. We gotta be careful that we don't get caught but us kids reckon it's worth the risk. Those old trees have got the biggest and nicest fruit you ever did see.

Usually, I play cockatoo (lookout) just in case Mr Pawsy or his sons are coming to check on his paddock. The bigger kids reckon I can't run as fast so I gotta sit on top of one of the fence posts and keep looking down the road for their car. I'll know it's him because the dust will be rising up into the air as he drives over the gutters and heads towards us. If I see him coming, I gotta yell real loud so we can run back home.

The boys will grab a handful of fruit each and Lynnie holds her shirt out like a basket and they fill it right up till she can't hold no more. Then we all head home and sit under our big old gum tree and start eating our rewards. After we've filled our faces, we all look at each other and laugh. The juice has run all down our mouths, making us look like babies dibbling. We even slobbered onto our shirts and blouses.

We all head inside after we've had our bellyful. We try to sneak inside on Mummy but I reckon she knows what we done.

She asks, 'You kids ain't been down where you shouldn't have been, have you?' She's looking straight at the four of us. I try to duck a little bit behind Paddy.

We tell her 'no' and then she tells us again, 'You know you're not allowed down there'.

All together we tell her, 'We know, Mummy'. Partners in crime forever. When Mummy's not looking, we sneak some figs and quinces onto the fruit bowl on the kitchen table so that everyone can share in our prize.

7

This old house

I reckon we got the best house on the Island. Lots of things happen there, good and bad. A real bad time was when I had to go to the hospital when I was about five and a half—it was terrible. They made me lie on a bed with this big, bright light over my head and then they put this white mask over my nose and mouth and then sprayed stuff onto it. I thought I was gonna die. They told me to close my eyes. I did, but then I opened them. I was terrified. There were all these people with masks over their faces standing over me. All I could see was these real big eyes looking at me. Then, this man was spraying me in the face and I'm screaming at the top of my lungs, trying to pull it off. I couldn't breathe but they grabbed my hands and held me down real tight.

I kept on trying to turn my head this way and that way, still trying to scream out for Mummy but they kept holding my arms and that mask against my face. Then, I don't remember nothing till I woke up and Mummy was sitting beside me.

I told Mummy, 'I don't ever wanna go back there again'.

She said not to worry, 'That's what doctors do to make you better'. Well, they musta made me better—I never went back. I'm always happiest at home on the Island.

There's always music in our house. The big girls gotta gramophone; the music is always playing, with lotsa fun and laughter. Meryl and Maureen can rock 'n' roll. Today, it's dancing time and Johnny, my biggest brother, and Meryl, my eldest sister, do the rock and roll steps for us. Johnny picks Meryl up and slides her over his back and underneath his legs, and they move their bodies to the sound of the music.

I sit back and watch, not taking my eyes off them for a minute, as they slip and slide all over the polished floorboards of our lounge room dancing away. I wanna dance like that!

After a while, we all get up and dance, even Mummy; she doesn't rock'n'roll like the big ones but she moves her body around. Soon, everyone is worn out from the fast music. Somebody changes the music on the gramophone and puts on slower music; we learn to dance to the waltz. I gotta stand on Mummy's shoes so she can teach me—'one, two, three, one, two, three'. Everybody swaps around so that we all have a dance with each other.

My big sisters, they know all the best songs; me and Lynnie, we know all the words, too. "North to Alaska", "Roses are Red", "Wolverton Mountain" and Elvis—they sing his songs, too. Always happiness is in our house, and laughing and singing. We're all pretty happy together unless the other kids tease me.

I've got wonderful big sisters, Meryl and Maureen, and they're so beautiful. They wear pretty dresses with hundreds of petticoats underneath. They tell us girls that when we get big, we can have dresses like them. They let me and Lynnie slip on a petticoat; it's made of net and scratches my skin but it doesn't matter. We both dance and prance, showing off and feeling real pretty and very happy. We both smile up to our big sisters, wanting so much to be like them.

They're good big sisters, too. They cut up their dresses so they can make clothes for us kids. Mummy made our Condo Show Day clothes out of the girls' old dresses. We all looked so beautiful and flash.

Sometimes, if Mummy has enough money, us younger ones are allowed to go to the pictures up the main street. She lets us go to the matinee show on the weekend by ourselves. One day, we watched a Shirley Temple movie. Maureen reckons I can have ringlets just like her. She rips up some brown paper and wraps it in my hair. All night, I slept with my hair in the brown paper. The next day, when Maureen takes the paper out of my hair, the ringlets didn't work. I got a head full of fuzzy hair instead. The kids call me a golliwog.

I start to cry and run to tell Mummy: 'I don't look like Shirley Temple'.

She gets Lynnie to wash my hair but it don't straighten up. Lynnie tells me she'll iron it straight for me. No way am I gonna let anyone iron my hair, especially with an old cast-iron iron that you have to heat up on the stove. She'll burn my hair off ! My hair went back to normal eventually but it took days. No more trying to look like Shirley Temple!

Each night, we all sit around in the lounge room and listen to the wireless. First, we gotta listen to the news, then it's music time. Everyone sings along to the songs that they play. Mummy, she can sing country and western and she can yodel, too, 'yodellllleettteeeee'. She even makes up songs as well but my favourite is when she sings the song about the frog.

A frog went a courtin' on a summer's day, ha-hum
A frog went a courtin' on a summer's day, ha-hum

There's lotsa fun and singing but Mummy's always working, too; she has to feed and clothe all us kids. We all have to pitch in and help do the jobs around the house. Mummy says, 'We all gotta learn how to do these things so, when we're grown up, we'll be able to look after ourselves'. Paddy, Lynnie and Kevin are bigger so they have real jobs to do but I do little jobs, too. We take it in turns. One night, the boys cut the wood and bring it in while us girls set the table and wash up. The next night, they set the table and wash up, then it's me and Lynnie's turn to do the wood.

I'm still only little so I'm not allowed to cut the wood yet but I help carry it in. Today, when it's our turn to get the wood, Lynnie tells me, 'Hold your hands out and bend them now, this way'. Starting to get angry, she plomps the wood onto my arms and the weight is getting to me.

Sometimes, Lynnie stacks the wood real high on my arms and its real heavy. When she does that, I try to tell her but she won't listen. I can't carry it so I usually drop it all halfway between the wood heap and the house. Then, she has to stack me again.

So, it's two trips to the house instead of one. Some days, she'll carry the other half for me, too. I don't mind carrying the wood but I can't wait till I'm big enough to be able to pick up the tomahawk and the axe, and swing them and split that wood in half.

I wipe when Lynnie washes up while the boys do their work outside. The best job we got is polishing the lounge-room floor and making the boards nice and shiny. I sit on the polishing rag so they can pull me around to shine the floor while I hang on to the sides with all my might so I don't fall over.

Depending on who's pulling me along, they even spin me around in circles! The boys do this real fast, trying to make me fall off. Sometimes, if I'm not hanging on real tight, over I go. Paddy, Lynnie and Kevin all take turns having a go at pulling each other. I try to help drag them around the room.

After the floor has been shined with our bums, we turn the music up real loud and we stand on a rag each, and we dance and glide all over the floor. We have races, too. We have a race to see who can make it to the other side of the lounge room first. I don't win that often since the other kids are quicker. Every now and then, they let me win and I think that I'm just it when they do that.

When we're finished playing and polishing, the floor always is real shiny and we can see our faces and bodies in it. When we're happy with it and had enough playing, we sing out to Mummy to come and have a look.

Lynnie puts Chubby Checker on the gramophone and we start doing the twist; Paddy pretends he has a microphone in his hands and starts singing to the song "Let's Twist Again". Kevin's twisting right down to the floor. Mummy stands at the door watching us, a big smile on her face. We show off when she's standing there.

She's happy. Her eyes twinkle and she says, 'What a great job you kids did'. She tells us she's got a surprise for us.

We follow her into the kitchen, and on the table, are some freshly made jam and apple tarts that she just pulled outta the old wood-fire oven. Our bellies are hungry all of a sudden. We sit down to pig-out on some of Mummy's wonderful cooking and a cup of Milo. Summer is here and, after a good feed and rest, we all head down to the best swimming spot in the Lachlan. We're happy kids. Life is good.

8

The silo and the Welfare Man

One time, during a flood, we stayed on the Island as long as we could, avoiding school, waiting for the water to go down. If the river floods, we gotta leave the Island but the Welfare reckons school is more important than staying put. When the river goes down, we come home again.

When the next flood happens, we go live in the tent up near the old silo beside the railway track. It's in town and not too far from the school and the shops, and there's a water tap there. Whenever we go live in the tent, we have to make sure that we can have clean drinking water.

The silo is big and old and dusty, and some kids have written inside and outside with paint; they mainly write their names. We use the silo for our playground and we sneak a look inside when Mummy's not looking. We always check to see if somebody has written something new on the walls while we were back living on the Island. We'd be in real trouble if Mummy caught us playing inside.

We're not allowed to play on the railway tracks either. It's dangerous and the trains are real fast and noisy. All we hear is a 'chug, chug, chug' and 'whooeee'—the sound of the whistle blowing. The tracks are so old they rattle as the train storms down the line. We don't have to worry about a clock. We can tell the time when the train comes by.

Mummy's got our spot for the tent. Putting us to work, we start picking up the sticks and stones to clear a spot for it to go up.

'Come on, you kids, you've gotta sweep all the leaves and stones up now,' she says.

Clutching the broom and leafy tree branches, we start to sweep away. Grabbing the buckets, Paddy and Kevin head to the tap to fill them up with water so we can sprinkle the dirt, settling it. No dust will fly around now. Laying the tent out in the middle of the clearing, we grab the corners and start to spread it out. The tent is huge!

All in a row, we sort out the tent posts, pegs and ropes, getting them ready to stick into the tent to hold it up. Mummy grabs the longest pole, putting the two ends together. The top looks like the teat on a baby's bottle. She finds the opening of the tent, shoving the pole with the teat end into its guts and sticking it out through the top hole—it begins to look like a tepee.

Her muscles ripple as she follows the pole inside the flaps, yelling out to Paddy to come inside and help hold it up. He runs inside and Mummy comes out so we can get the ropes and pegs in. The tent starts to buckle in the middle, but Paddy quickly rights it again. It would have fell on him if he had let it go.

'Hold the post tight, Paddy,' Mummy sings out.

'I'm trying to,' he yells in reply. She sends Kevin in to help him.

Hooking the rope over the top of the side posts, she pulls each rope tight. Lynnie and me run and help, holding the tent while she pounds the posts into place with the hammer. Soon, she calls out to the boys and they help pull the ropes tighter into the dirt. The tent is firmly placed.

Dragging in our clothes and some old tea boxes, we begin to make our tent a home—working out where the kitchen and beds go is fun. Our cupboards and drawers are made from the tea boxes that have tablecloths draped over them so they look real nice and people can't tell what they are. Covered over, the box quickly becomes our kitchen; a dish for our washing up is close by. The pots and pan are stored together with the plates, bowls, knives, forks and spoons into other boxes.

Paddy strings some rope down the middle of the tent and Mummy lays a sheet over it, dividing the room. She's a real stickler for privacy. The boys have a bed each on their side of the tent and Mummy and Lynnie have a bed each, too. I sleep at the foot of Mummy's bed. I don't mind—I don't need my own bed. She reads each night as she waits for us kids to fall asleep. She doesn't read too long as candles are expensive and she don't like them being wasted.

We've been living in the tent next to the silo for a while now and the Welfare man, he's coming today, checking up on us. Mummy tells us how important it is for us to be real good in front of him and that everything's gotta be spotless. The tent is spick and span. There's not one thing out of place. I don't know why she worries, it's always clean, anyway. Mummy, she's real neat and tidy and us kids are, too. We make our beds, wash up, wipe up and put things away.

She tells me to be good when he's here and to have nice manners like the other kids who have gone to school. We always have nice manners anyway and are always good. I wonder what the fuss is all about.

Mummy gets the straw broom this day and sweeps our dirt floor inside the tent. She fills a bucket of water and sprinkles water over the dirt to stop the dust rising. Us kids sweep the dirt outside around the tent, picking up any leaves or rubbish. I love the smell of the water on the dirt. It smells like when it rains. I have fun sprinkling the water but I think I made more puddles than sprinkles.

The Welfare man comes and goes, and she tells us we're good kids. We all smile and feel real proud of ourselves, each one of us wanting and needing her praise. I think we're good kids, too, except when the others tease me. We know the importance of having to be good, especially when we hear the word 'Welfare'. Somehow, we know life's hard enough as it is without having the Welfare knocking on our door. Living in fear of the Welfare quickly becomes a part of my young life, even though I don't really understand why.

I ask Lynnie who is the Welfare, but she just says, 'Don't worry about it'.

She thinks I'm too little and wouldn't understand. I get real mad when they do that to me, treating me like a baby. I wanna know. I yell at her and stamp my foot; she tells me that she'll tell me later when no one's around.

Later, Lynnie tells me a horrible thing: the Welfare man, he can take us away from Mummy if the house isn't spotless or if we aren't going to school or even if we muck up. He can take us away just if he feels like it! She says he can do whatever he wants. He doesn't need any reason and no one can stop him—not even Mummy.

She tells me I'd better be good or the Welfare will come and take me away. I tell her I'll always be good—I don't wanna go anywhere. I just wanna stay here with my family.

It's different living in town and living in a tent. The shops are closer so we don't have to walk down the gutters day or night, but we all wanna go home. The Island's the best place. We all wait for the day Mummy says we can go home to the Island—home to where we belong.

One day, the other kids go to school and, when they come back to the tent, Mummy and me are packing our things up. The river's gone down again. Time to shift home.

9

Going home to the Island

Happiness! We're back on the Island in our house. Now, I can play with my toys and my dolls. I tell the house I'm glad to be home. I'm sure the house is happy we're home, too. It's okay in the tent but you wouldn't wanna live in one for the rest of your life.

I'm getting big now, just like the other kids, and that means it's school time. They still boss me around and tease me but they look after me when they take me to school and back. As we walk there, they say, if anyone gives me a hard time, I gotta tell them and they will take care of the other kids and make them stop. I'm so happy I got this big sister and these big brothers that look after me; I wouldn't want them not to be my family. I feel safe and protected by my Mob.

At the school, I got lotsa friends, too, as well as cousins. There's a group of us kids that hang out together: there's Dottie and Denise Whiting, Keith Brandy and Ally Coe, Johnny Huckle and Loretta Sloane and a few more, too. All us Aboriginal kids play together.

When Mummy dresses us girls for school, we gotta look good, the boys, too, but us girls especially. She makes sure we're all clean and tidy and neat with our uniform. We gotta have our shoes and socks on; we wouldn't be game to go to school with no shoes on. Our uniform has to be pressed every Sunday and the boys have gotta polish all our shoes.

Mummy puts bobby pins in me and Lynnie's hair. The pins hurt our heads and we hate them. We know there's not much sense telling Mummy we don't want them in our hair—she'd make us wear them anyway. We wait till we get down the gutters and take them out and hide them under a rock.

We go to school with our hair flying everywhere, a mess, but we don't care. We get the bobby pins on the way home and slip them back into our hair, trying to remember exactly how Mummy stuck them in that morning. Every day, she shoves them in and, every day, we take them right out again.

We always gotta look good: our faces washed, shoes and socks on, clothes ironed. We don't give nobody any reason to talk about us. In my mind, I still can't fully understand the reasons why. I'm still too young to know that being taken away by the Welfare is a constant risk.

It's the weekend so we head down the gutters. It's our secret place, our playground, our hiding spot. It's the whole world to us. We plant our favourite things in the gutters under the rocks but we gotta make sure the rivers not gonna come up first. One time, Paddy hid some pound notes down there, under a big rock, but the river came up during the night and washed them away! He swore all the next day. It was a good thing Mummy didn't hear him or he would've copped it. She was very strong on us not swearing. It was another way to draw attention to us and our whole lives had to be about not drawing white people's attention to our family.

10

'Your mother's dead'

I like school. I reckon it's pretty good; I got lotsa friends and cousins. And at recess, you get a bottle of milk and an apple. The teacher said an apple a day keeps the doctor away, and one day, I went home and told Mummy. She reckoned that was true.

Another day, it's recess and I'm hanging around with a group of kids playing hopscotch. One of the girls didn't like me beating her. She couldn't jump as far as me and so she started yelling at me.

'Your mother's dead, your mother's dead.'

I scream at her and tell them Mummy's at work.

'She's not dead, she's working!'

They tell me, 'No, not her, your other mother'. I don't understand. Then, somebody says, 'Your real mother's dead—your father killed her'. I call them liars and run away. I don't want to listen no more. I run away to the girls' toilets, trying to stop crying, but tears slowly run down my cheeks. I wonder why they would be so mean and tell me such lies but, somehow, I know it's true. Deep down, I know they're not lying. My heart tries not to break and my mind tries not to think.

I don't want another mother. I only want Mummy. She's my mother. I sit on the toilet, sobbing. In my childish mind, I somehow know that I really did have another mother who is now dead, but in my make-believe, there was this other mother who died saving us kids in the war. The story I tell myself goes like this:

She died while she was trying to get away from the bombs, trying to save our lives. She was even trying to save me and all the other kids, passing us down to Mummy before it was her turn to go down into the bomb shelter. I can see her so clearly. Her hair like mine, she's wearing a real pretty white dress with little tiny flowers on it and petticoats underneath.

I sit there quiet. All of a sudden, I feel nothing. Only the feeling that she's dead.

My mind is a jumble, just like my heart. They musta got it wrong, got me mixed up with someone else. The teacher finds me in the toilet, crying. I just wanna go home. They send for Lynnie to come and quieten me, but she can't.

I tell her between my sobs, 'I wanna go home, I want Mummy!'

She takes me with her to her classroom but I can't stop crying so they let her take me home. She takes me up to where Mummy's working as a cook. Lynnie tells her she had to bring me home from school as I was crying real bad. She tells her to take me home and look after me. When Mummy comes back from work, I tell her.

'I don't want to go to school anymore.'

'You gotta go to school. Everyone has to go.'

'But Mummy, the kids don't like me.'

'Don't worry about them.'

My mind screams inside but I don't say nothing to Mummy. I keep telling myself my mother died in an air raid in the war. My father didn't kill her. I couldn't have a father who would be so bad as to kill somebody. I try to smile and pretend to be happy.

When I lie in my bed at night, I can't sleep. Images run through my head. I picture her in my mind going into a tunnel down in the dirt.

I see her starting to climb down the ladder. She's stepping in, being real careful not to slip or fall. She makes sure we're all down into the air raid shelter. I can just see her. She stands. The lid is covered with branches so the baddies can't see it, and then, nothing. SHE'S GONE.

She died. Daddy fought in the war. So did Uncle Raymond, Uncle Paddy and Uncle Athol. I tell myself, 'No, she died in the war'. That's what I'll tell them kids, too, if they say those terrible things again. A mother that died in the war. I will say she was a hero. She saved people and that's why she died.

I don't wanna have a mother who is dead or a father who killed her, but in my heart, I know. There are things in my family I'm not allowed to hear, not allowed to know. When the grown-ups are talking, we gotta go outside. We know they're gonna talk about things that's real important.

Mummy makes sure we don't know grown-up things. She reckons we should be kids for as long as we can. She'd have told them all—my bigger brothers and sisters and all our family—she would've said they weren't allowed to talk about these things to us.

I go back to school. I try to stay away from those terrible kids but it's hard since we all play together. Soon they don't say nothing about dead people or people dying. After a while, all the memories of other mothers and fathers are gone from my six-year-old head.

11

Living at the cemetery

It's that time of year. The river's up again so we go back to making our bridge with our rocks and walking through water every day for the kids to get to school. Splashing and playing around, we chase each other to see who can get the best rocks first. I'm getting bigger and I can pick up larger ones now, and I'm real proud of myself. Each day, we add a few more rocks. Each of us kids pray that the river doesn't flood this year so we don't have to leave the Island and camp in the tent in town.

It doesn't take long, though, before the river is rushing over our little bridge. I'm too big now to get on Mummy's shoulder. She tried to put me up there but I was too heavy. Last time, I'm sure I felt her body crumble a little bit when I got on top. She tried to take a few steps but just couldn't.

She had to put me down. Now, I gotta wade across like the other kids. There's a belt around her waist and she makes me hook my hand in and then she tightens the belt over it. Wrapping her hand around mine, she hangs on tight making sure my other hand doesn't slip outta hers.

She goes back and brings the others over. Then, we all play cockatoo again while we all get dressed before heading up Bathurst Street into the town.

Days go past and soon the river's too high so it's time for us to move off the Island. Us kids moan and groan about going back to the silos and the train tracks. We're all tired of the train rattling down the tracks and blowing its whistle. Mummy looks for somewhere else; no matter where it is, we know, eventually, we will be back on the Island real soon.

Mummy's found a new place to pitch the tent! We pack our swag and head out. She doesn't tell us where it is, saying it's a surprise. This time, we're going to live a heartbeat from the graves! Take a big step and you're there; the graves are our neighbours.

She's found us a spot near the fence, kinda hidden from the road, with gum trees and bushes. My childish mind sees the graves hover over our tent, a skip and a jump for me to fall into when my bigger brothers and sister are teasing me but most likely it is positioned along the fence at the far end of the cemetery away from the graves. She puts us to work picking up the sticks and stones to clear a spot for the tent to go up. Quickly, we all jump in and give a hand and it's done.

The tea boxes and beds go in, and soon we are all set up again. We have the routine down pat: drape the tablecloth and tea towels over the boxes and no one would ever know. Paddy grabs the rope to make a divider up the middle of the tent for privacy between all of us. Mummy reminds us kids we always have to be dressed before dark as people can see our shadows and she doesn't want anyone to see us putting our pyjamas on—otherwise, we have to do it in the dark.

Walking through the graves, we go and fill up our water buckets from the tap. It's the one that people use to fill up their flower vases to put on the graves. It's a fair way from the tent. It's Paddy and Kevin's job to make sure our water buckets are full but us girls gotta take our turn carting the water, too. At dark, it's really scary; we always try to make sure that we fill our water buckets before nightfall and we're careful not to be disrespectful to the dead.

As the night closes in, Mummy lights a candle and asks, 'who wants to play cards?' Shuffling the deck, she deals a hand to each of us; we all take a turn dealing. Playing for matches is great and, somehow, we all win. None of us ever realised Mummy cheated, making sure that we all had plenty of matches for the next day's game. During the weekend, we play jacks, marbles and hide'n-go-seek when we are not at school.

It's not bad living at the cemetery. We walk around and read the headstones, and there's some pretty ones with angels and things carved into them. Some of the graves are real bare and look so sad with not even a flower on them; they look lost and alone. A lot have got no crosses and some are even as flat as a pancake, and many are very old—they're ancient.

On Sundays, we gotta tend to our family's graves and we help look after other people's graves, too. Like the ones where, if the flowers have fallen off, we put them back in the vase and, standing it up, we make it look good. We know where most of our family are buried. There's not too many of our Mob who has angels and headstones. Most of our family's graves just have little white crosses and a lot of flowers.

I feel sorry for the ones that look lost and lonely. They're the graves that nobody loves anymore and are forgotten about. When I ask Mummy why they don't get visitors, she tells me, 'All their families might not be around anymore'. Even she feels sad for those ones. She tells us to pick some wildflowers and fill up the empty jars or the Sunshine milk tin and place them on the graves.

On dusk, we run around finding sticks to put on our fire, the boys dragging back big, broken-down branches. Each night, we huddle around the fire as Mummy cooks our tucker and the heat glows on our faces. The fire is burning bright and we're happy. We're letting the spirits know we're here; we're being respectful.

There's no train whistle tooting here; it's much quieter than beside the railway track. I reckon people think we're mad to be living here and that's why they don't come near us, especially at night. All day, we hear the birds singing and, at night, we hear the night animals hooting and creeping around. When the wind is rustling the leaves from the trees, it's really spooky. I pull the blanket right over my head and close my eyes real tight some nights.

There's no streetlight near us so, as night closes in, it's pitch-black outside the tent, especially when the stars aren't shining or the moon is covered with clouds. I'm happy we got our fire; we keep it stacked high with logs so it gives us plenty of light to see by.

Some nights when we're sitting outside around the fire, the boys and Lynnie chuck stones to make a noise to scare me. I turn my head to see where the noise has come from, straining my eyes to see if I can see anything white out there amongst the trees and the graves.

'Look, Kerry, there's something over there.'

'Where?'

'Over there, look.'

I turn my head to see, so miss seeing another stone thrown. They try to boss me around and tell me, 'You've gotta go and see what it is'.

'No, I don't.'

'Yes, you do.'

Clinging to the chair I'm sitting on, they try to push me towards the noise. I don't wanna go and see no spirits! I'm off the chair ready to run inside to Mummy but I feel a hand push me in the back, pushing me in the direction of the noise. I'm one step closer to a grave, one step closer to being near the spirits. I'm scared, deep down inside! There really might be spirits out there and they might decide to keep me, then I would have no family anymore! I scream out to Mummy! She comes from outta the tent and tells them to leave me alone.

She tells me, 'You don't have to be scared of the dead ones, daught, only the live ones'.

I don't take much notice of the others now I know no spirit can take me away. Only the Welfare.

Part Two

12

Back on the Island

We're heading home once again and this old house of ours looks better each time we come back from living in the tent. We're all happy, back where we belong. One day, we catch brother Paddy smoking down in the gutters. He can make circles with the smoke. My eyes are wide as I watch him take a deep breath and move his mouth just right to make a perfect circle escape between his lips.

Lynnie tells him, 'We're gonna tell Mummy'.

He reckons, 'No way', and makes us smoke a cigarette.

He tells us, 'If we don't do it properly the first time, we gotta do it again'.

Lynnie, being the next eldest, has to go first.

Paddy says, 'Take a big breath. Draw back.'

Then, it's Kevin's turn. I watch them each having a go drawing back on that smoke, only to end up coughing, with tears coming outta their eyes, and then Paddy passing the smoke to them again so they can have another go.

It's my turn. I take a draw but it's not big enough, the smoke doesn't make me cough the way it did with the other two. He makes me do it again. I take a big breath this time and smoke goes deep into my mouth all the way down to my lungs and I start choking, tears in my eyes. I can't catch my breath. Lynnie is patting me on the back trying to get all that smoke outta my lungs. Tears are dripping outta my eyes.

Paddy says, 'Now we've all smoked, we can't tell Mummy. Otherwise, we'll all be in trouble.'

It's Saturday, the sun is shining and us four kids are allowed to go to the pictures, all by ourselves. The picture's great: it's Elvis. I love Elvis but I don't like the lion that comes out and roars real loud, and you can see his big teeth. I don't tell the others this, otherwise they'll make my life a misery teasing me again.

We walk home laughing and talking about Elvis, trying to remember his songs. We sing "Love Me Tender" all the way home.

We laugh and giggle about the show and the cartoons, all as happy as can be. We walk down to the end of the main street and start down the dirt track that leads us home to the Island. Mainly, we go to the matinee show, but as we get older, we're allowed to go to the night shows. That's good but frightening, too. At night, the gutters are scary. Scary, dark and noisy. Spirits live down there. At the end of the main street, there's no streetlights—only the stars and the moon to guide us—but we know this road well. We start talking loud, making a noise to let the spirits know we're coming home.

As we get deeper down into the gutters, the bigger kids start singing, 'Jesus loves me this I know, for the Bible tells me so'. I join in. We're in the middle of the gutters now. Our voices are softer as we sing a song about the devil.

The devil is a sly old fox and, if I catch him,

I'll put him in a box, lock the door and throw away the key for all the tricks he played on me.
I'll do it all for Jesus, I'll do it all for Jesus,
He's done so much for me.

There's a rustling coming from over in that tree. The bigger kids start teasing me.

'Oooooh, Kerry, you wanna watch out: they're watchin' you!'

'They're comin' to get you. Listen, here they come.'

A noise comes out loud from amongst the trees. I look and see shadows; shadows that appear as ghosts waiting to get me and take me away. The wind is blowing the branches and it really does sound like someone or something is standing there, waiting for the right moment to jump out and get me. The other kids start screaming out at the top of their lungs, pretending the ghost is right there, right beside me. They start running at the same time.

'They gonna get you!'

'There's one right behind you, Kerry!'

Terrified, I stand still, not wanting to take another step. I want Mummy. I'm scared and alone and it's dark. Paralysed, I stand and watch three bodies run up the top of the gutters; they've left me behind! I'm in the middle of the gutters by myself. I start screaming as I watch my sister and brothers leave me and feel the wind encase my body as I would a spirit taking hold of me. I start to run, bolting as fast as my legs will carry me while trying to catch them and swearing at the same time.

'Don't leave me!'

'Don't let them get me!'

Sobbing, I run up the other side of the gutters but I can't catch up. I can't breathe. I can't run no more. I stop, willing air to come back into my lungs so I can begin to scream and yell. I scream at them at the top of my lungs, 'I'm gonna tell Mummy'.

They stop, wait. My favourite and best saying, 'I'm gonna tell Mummy'.

They call me a sook and say I'd better not dob them in, otherwise I'm gonna cop it. And they won't take me to see Elvis again.

When we get home, Mummy asks, 'What was all the noise down in the gutters?' They all look at me, daring me to tell on them, but I don't—know they'll get me if I do. And I don't really wanna get them into trouble.

I say, 'Nothing, Mummy. We was just singing.'

I didn't tell, but they still leave me down the gutters every time we go to the pictures. Scaring me to death. I love Elvis so much. If we got no money, the kids aren't allowed to tell me if Elvis is on at the pictures. If they do, I wanna go so bad that I chuck a big tantrum and I cry and scream out at the top of my lungs about going to see him. One day, to keep me quiet, Mummy told me I was gonna go to the blanket show instead of the picture show. I was so happy.

I asked her, 'What's the blanket show?'

She tells me, 'It's a surprise, but if you hurry up, brush your teeth and put your pyjamas on, then you'll find out'.

I run and do my teeth and change into my pyjamas and then I'm back, quick as lightening.

'I'm ready, Mummy,' I tell her, and then she gets up and takes me into my bedroom and tells me to get into bed so she can tuck me in. I start crying.

'I wanna go to the blanket show.'

'Come on, then. This is the blanket show. You go to bed.'

The kids start laughing, teasing me. I'm angry and upset—I wanted to go to the picture show not the lousy blanket show. I don't wanna go there; I wanna go to the pictures and see Elvis!

All the next day, the other kids tease and tease: 'Kerry, you wanna go to the blanket show?'

I hate them. They're always tormenting me. As soon as I get something wrong or do something dumb, they give me heaps.

13

Daddy's home

Daddy's home. He's been gone a long time but he's back and he's got presents for all us kids. He brought me a pair of red boots and he's brought lots of lollies, too. The boots are so pretty and just right—I won't take them off. Mummy's worried Daddy spent most of his pay on lollies and presents. He stays for a little bit, then he's off to work once more. He must see lots of the bush as he pumps up and down on the little railway machine. We don't see him again for a while.

Each Sunday night, we get our school clothes ready. Heating up the old iron on the stove fire, Mummy presses our uniforms. It's called a serge uniform and the pleats are hard to do—you've gotta get the lines perfect. We have to wrap a tea towel around the handle when it's hot enough to do the job, otherwise it would burn our hands when we grabbed it. Lynnie irons the house clothes and I'm allowed to iron the hankies and tea towels when the iron's cooled down a bit.

Some nights, Mummy will do all the ironing if she's not worn out but I reckon she must get pretty buggered sometimes. She never stops and that's why us kids gotta help with the house and our chores. Mummy and Aunty Doris (Mummy's big sister), they always work like a man because they have to—sometimes, men's work is the only work they can get to feed all us kids. I hear stories of her and Aunty Doris going stick-picking to feed all us kids and how they had to walk for a mile to get to work and back again. That's where all the bigger kids came in handy, helping to mind us little ones. Aunty Doris has a lot of kids; she's married to Uncle Clyde.

Life on the Island is happy. Maureen is gonna marry Sam. I'm a little kid about six and a half but Maureen is nearly seventeen at this stage (she's ten years older than me). We all get special clothes to wear. Kevin and Paddy each have a suit with a little bow tie, while me and Lynnie get a pretty dress. I get one with a petticoat.

Maureen tells us girls how pretty we look and so does Mummy. We all pose for photos, smiling up real big. We feel so good in our special clothes.

But it turns out we got the clothes for nothing because us four younger kids aren't allowed to go to the wedding. They said no kids were allowed. Again, I hear whispers about us not being real brothers and sisters and that's why. Some people are so dumb—we're all brothers and sisters and I'm the baby, don't they know that? Boy, people can make you so mad, especially when they don't know what they're talking about.

Mummy tells us we can wear our special clothes to the Condo Show instead, which is soon. The Condo Show is the best thing that happens each year. It's got lotsa rides, showbags and fairy floss; I love the Cha-Cha ride the best. One of the bigger kids has to get on there with me because it goes fast and I'll fly off if I'm by myself.

Every time I line up with Lynnie and Kevin to get on that Cha-Cha, I try to remember what side not to sit on so that I can squash the other kids. But no matter how much I try, I always get it wrong and it's always me getting squashed. Every year I make a vow that one day when I'm bigger, I'm gonna squash them and then they can yell at the top of their lungs. Paddy's grown now so he can go on the bigger and faster rides. We only see him when he comes to check on us or to give us some extra spending money if he's won any. He's good for sharing what he's got with us younger ones.

Maureen lives down the road from us now. Her and Sam live with Sam's parents in the house down near the water pump. We miss her a lot, especially when our big brothers come around and give us a hard time. They like to pick on Paddy and Kevin more than me and Lynnie. Paddy's in trouble today. I don't know what he's done; I only know he's gonna get it real bad. Me and Kevin run down the road for Maureen. Lynnie stays, trying to help Paddy, but us four younger kids are no match for the big ones.

We all know that Maureen tries to protect us and fights with the big boys if they threaten to give us a flogging if they think one of us has been bad or done something wrong. Today, we gotta save Paddy. We run down to Maureen's house, screaming for her to help save us—she has to stop the hiding. We run down there as fast as we can, screaming out at the top of our lungs before we have even made it into the gate. She runs back with us, her pregnant belly running before her; she knew the urgency was there. Today, she wins and there's no hiding for Paddy. They never pick on us when Mummy's around.

And, sometimes, our big brothers are really mean for no reason; so we hate it when Maureen goes away from the Island because we've got no one to protect us from them when Mummy's at work. Meryl would protect us but she's away in Bible College.

If Mummy found out the big boys were giving us a hard time, she'd be angry. If we're really bad, we only get a hiding off Mummy. I ain't never got a hiding yet but, if she's cranky with us kids, then we gotta do extra chores like cut a stack of wood or something. If it's me she's cranky with, I gotta help the boys wash up, even if it's not my turn.

When we've done something real bad, then we gotta go and pick a stick from the tree and bring it back inside. We gotta test that stick to make sure it has a swoosh sound. If it don't make a swoosh noise, then we've gotta pick another one. I think she just does that to scare us; I don't think any of us ever got the stick.

We go on being happy living on the Island and, for us kids, its back to normal: school, Mummy working hard and us trying to be good so the Welfare can't take us away.

14

Happy Christmas

It's 1963 and I'm seven years old. Opening the back door,

I hear the wireless going. Mummy's been crying; John F. Kennedy, a good man, has died. She says that he was trying to make things better for the Black people over in America and that we need somebody like that here in Australia—somebody who would stand up and be counted for Aboriginal people. The wireless gets turned off and we're not allowed to play; we gotta show respect.

Soon after that, I gotta go to Sydney to the doctor's to get my tonsils and adenoids out, all in one go. Mummy takes me up there herself, just us two. I get plenty of ice cream to eat and Mummy sits at my bed, waiting patiently for me to get better; for the doctor to tell her I can go home.

I don't remember much about the train ride up there but I sure had a good train ride home. In Sydney, we find Johnny's future wife, Beryl, and her baby boy. His name is Raymond but I call him Nay, and he is lovely. They are travelling home with us. The train is an old one that rattles along the track, but I like the sound, rattle, rattle, rattle. The seats are real leather, real soft to sit on. Above the seat, are rails that hold our luggage; they're all gold and shiny. I ask Mummy if it's real gold and she tells me, no. Mummy lets me have the window seat and gives me sandwiches to eat. She tells me that, when the train stops, she'll buy me a drink and a lolly.

I ask for my turn to hold Nay, every now and then; he's a good baby and happy. I pull funny faces at him and make him smile. I sit and look out the window. First, I see all the houses go past then, all of a sudden, there's nothing but trees. It's so lovely out there. I love looking at all the trees rushing past you real fast. I tell Mummy she's gotta have a look out the window. And she does.

I see her reflection in the glass and she looks so pretty, saying we have the most beautiful country in the world. I sit and watch the miles go by as the train takes me back to my brothers and sisters. I've missed them so much, even if they tease me. I just wanna go home now, to the Island.

Beryl's in love with my brother, Johnny, and they're gonna get married. That means her and Nay are gonna be a part of my family. I'm happy we've got two new babies now. Maureen's little boy, we call him Bo, was born in October, three days after my birthday, so I've become an Aunty two times and I'm still only seven years old. We are so lucky. They both get very spoilt; me and Lynnie play with them instead of our dolls now.

I'm getting big. Now I'm allowed to cut the pine wood to light the fire. Lynnie has to watch me while she gets to cut the big wood. I've gotta use the tomahawk, Mummy said. I'm too little yet to use the big axe by myself, but I don't mind. Soon, I know I'm gonna swing that axe and I bet I can cut the big wood just as good as the boys.

It's cherry-picking time but I'm still sick. Mummy and the other kids are gonna go and pick the fruit without me, and I'm staying here on the Island with Aunty Carol and Uncle Paddy. They're gonna watch the house and me. It's okay but I wish I'd gone picking. If my stupid tonsils didn't have to come out, I would've been able to go. The paddock is ten times better than staying home; I love picking cherries and, best of all, I love climbing the trees. My favourite spot is right up the fork of the tree to the highest branch where I can stand and look out at the world.

Mummy and the kids finally come home from the cherry picking. I run out to the car and jump into my mother's arms, kissing her, holding onto her for dear life. Finally, she unwinds her body from my arms and I give my brothers and sister a kiss and a cuddle. I'm so happy. I tell her I don't ever want her to leave me again; I've missed them all so much.

She asks whether everything was all right while she was gone. I tell her, 'Yes'. Everything was good and it was. And even if it wasn't, I know better now than to say a bad word about anybody, otherwise they'll tell Mummy I was naughty and she'll send me away, and the Welfare will come and take me. I hate the Welfare.

It's Christmas Day and all the family is here. I'm so happy! Santa brought me lots of things, lots of clothes and I've got a doll's cradle. My bride doll fits just perfect.

Mummy and the big girls have been cooking real hard all day. They have been slaving over that old wood stove for hours. Perspiration was dripping off them, and walking into the kitchen from outside, the heat knocks you rotten. The smell of a baked dinner with lotsa goodies has been teasing our noses all morning—we know a big feast is about to happen.

Christmas! I love all the presents and all the tucker, but I love the lollies the best. Mummy puts lollies out so us kids can have some whenever we want, even before dinner. There's peanuts and chips and licorice allsorts and bullets and cobbers—all our favourites, spread out on the table waiting for us to eat, eat and enjoy. We're so lucky.

Mummy said we're not to make ourselves sick from eating too many and we had to save room for Christmas dinner; but she doesn't know that the boys take lots and put them in their pockets 'cause they're pigs. Mummy and the girls bring out all the food. There's everything: a baked leg, a chook, baked potatoes and pumpkin and lots more. Everybody's around the table; we're a big family. We all pile around, making sure we can all fit in, but we didn't have to worry—the table's big enough to hold us all.

A special Christmas pudding was made by Mummy and it's got sixpences and threepences in it. All us kids are hoping our piece of pudding has a coin. I'm getting close to the end of mine and I can't see any. I don't reckon I got one, not even a threepence. I feel my bottom lip quiver, close to tears at the thought that I was gonna miss out. She reaches over (slipping a coin in) and tells me to wait till I've finished and to have a closer look. I try to stop the tears from springing to my eyes and look real hard at my last spoonful of pudding, willing a coin to be there, just waiting for me to find. Mummy was right, I've gotta a coin and it's a sixpence.

I show my coin to everyone and tell them all how rich I am, and that I'm gonna buy some lollies up at Wright Heaton's and maybe even something at Chamen's. All us kids got a coin and we all talk at once on what we're gonna buy. It's not that often we get to be so rich together. Christmas day is real special, too; us younger kids don't have to do no work. No washing up, wiping up or even cutting wood—it's our day off. All we gotta do is be good and play together out the front. We play lotsa games together, like rounders, "Simon says", "pick up sticks". Even Mummy and the other grown-ups come out to play with us. Christmas day; the best day of all.

***

Boxing Day. That's pretty good, too; that's another family day. It's the day that all the ones who couldn't come yesterday, come. We all head down to the riverbank, the part where we cart our water from. We have a great family corroboree and light a fire to cook our tucker on; and we all play games and we fish and relax.

Finding two dead stumps and a piece of tin, the boys make us a barbecue—the tin is to put on top of the wood to cook the meat. Us kids gotta run up and down the riverbank and find wood to keep the fire going. Mummy and the girls start the cooking. Me, I'm just waiting for the meat to be cooked. I love the sausages and chops cooked on that old piece of tin with lots of tomato sauce and onions wrapped between a slice of fresh bread. It makes my seven-year-old belly so happy.

While the women cook the tucker, the men make the fishing lines for us kids. Each of us has to find a stick that's strong enough to use. It's like a race: we all line up, and on the count of three, start running till we find the perfect stick. For some reason, we all start running in the same direction, heading to the same tree. Usually, the big kids get there first and us little ones gotta go and find another tree with some sticks under it. That's not hard to do; the trees line up, side by side, guarding the riverbank so there's plenty for us to choose from.

Bringing our sticks back to the men, they wrap just enough fishing line on the stick and where the cork, hook and sinker needs to be. All the bigger kids are lined up in front of me, getting theirs made. I stand impatiently, waiting for them to hurry up so I can chuck my line in, too.

When all the lines are made, we race along the riverbank picking out our favourite fishing spot. We run fast, trying to make sure no one beats us to it. We gotta be careful there's no snags in the water. If there's a tree branch sticking outta the water where you wanna fish, you know that spot's no good. If you chuck your line out where there's snags, when you pull it back in, you'll break your line and lose your hook and sinker. We can't chuck our line in where our water pump is either, otherwise we'd get a snag for sure.

Us kids aren't allowed to go too far away from the grownups so we're all spread out along the riverbank with just enough room between us not to get the lines tangled up when we chuck them out. It's my favourite time of all, sitting on the riverbank, chucking that line in, just sitting there watching the water ripple in with the current and feeling the sun beaming right down on you. I reckon this is what heaven would be like.

We always race to see who can catch the first fish. Whoever gets him first always gets a surprise. I cross my fingers hoping it's me. I wanna catch a big yellow belly, the best fish in the world. I don't want no catfish to jump on my line. Mummy says we don't eat it, so we don't—I think it's a cultural tradition but I don't really know. Our fish is the yellow belly; we can eat that one and it tastes good.

This spot is where we go swimming, too, and our learn-to-swim school when one of the little kids has gotta learn. Us older kids and some of the grown-ups form a circle out in the river and one of the men will chuck each one into the water in the middle of us all and they gotta swim back to the riverbank.

I hear the male voice go *one, two,* and then we all yell *three* together. I feel the splash and the river wash over me, nearly drowning me. I scrape the water from my face and hold my breath, waiting and watching, willing them to start dog-paddling. The grown-ups all watch to make sure everything's okay. When each kid has reached the riverbank, we all start clapping and hawhooing.

It's down here at this same spot that we cart our water from; the pump's just over near the trees and there's a tap on it. We carry our water up to the house. I'm too little to carry full buckets but I gotta help Lynnie. We try to carry them between us on a stick like the Chinese do—with a stick over our shoulders and a metal bucket on each end—but that didn't work 'cause I was too short. We gotta concentrate real hard when we're carrying the buckets back so that we don't spill all of our water. Otherwise, we gotta turn around and come back and do it all over again. It's really hard yakka, and Lynnie takes big steps. When I get bigger, I can carry a full bucket home by myself.

The bigger kids have got to reach into the river and fill the buckets up and pass them up to us littler ones. Mummy said there was no way I was to try to fill the bucket up myself. But one day, I did and slipped on the mud and fell right into that river, without even making a great big splash.

The current took me down deep under the surface. I could see Lynnie—she had her back to me, putting her bucket down, and I was trying to swim back up to her but I couldn't. The water was rushing all over me. My eyes were wide open and I felt I was moving in slow motion. I must've been splashing about because the next thing you know, Lynnie pulled me up by the hair. We didn't tell Mummy—she would've been angry at us both; me for going down to the edge of the riverbank when I knew I wasn't allowed and Lynnie for letting me. I had a lucky escape from disaster that day, for sure, but what nobody knew was that another disaster was waiting for our family, just over the horizon.

Mummy at the age of 17 in Griffith, 1941.

Goma, Kerry's birth mother, when she met Kevin Gilbert in 1954.

Kevin with the birds, Heckle and Jeckle, in Trundal, 1957.

L to R: Kevin, Lynnie and Kerry playing marbles on the Island, 1958.

Kerry and Kevin, Condobolin Show Day, 1961.

Kerry holding her bride doll, 1964.

Last Christmas dinner on the Island before the family house burnt down, 1963.

Kevin, second row, second from right, in Condobolin, 1965.

Kerry, far left, second row from back, wearing a serge uniform, Koorawatha, 1968.

Mormon baptism day at Murrumbidgee River in Leeton. Back row, L to R: Lynnie, Elder Hadley and Paddy. Front row: Bobby Smith (Sam's brother), Kevin, Kerry and their cousin Billy Bell (Uncle Paddy's son), 1966.

Mummy and Uncle Paddy Naden picking oranges, Leeton, 1970.

Mummy picking cherries, Young, 1972.

Kerry's birth father, Kevin Gilbert, and Mummy in Kooringhat, 1976.

Daddy and Meryl, Christmas in Cessnock, 1981.

Kerry and her father, Kevin Gilbert, celebrating her daughter, Lesa's 17th birthday in Ainslie, 1991.

Kerry's graduation day, Bachelor Adult Education majoring in Community Development and Aboriginal Education, UTS, 1995.

Kerry and brother Kevin at Mummy's 80th birthday in Parkes, 2004.

Mummy on a swing in Watson, 1999.

Mummy's 80th birthday in Parkes. Back row, L to R: Kevin, Kerry, Paddy and Lynnie. Front row: Mummy and Meryl surrounded by great grandchildren, 2004.

Kerry and her daughters, Lesa and Melanie, in Downer, ACT, 2015.

Kerry and her grandchildren in Downer. Back row, L to R: Jirrima and Yarran. Front row, L to R: Tenisha, Kaylarnie and Yullara, 2015.

15

1964: my Island home all gone

In February, we would head out to pick the oranges at Leeton. We had a good picking season this year and now we're heading back home to the Island. I'm in the front of the ute with Mummy and Daddy; he's home again and helped us pick this year. The other three kids are in the back. We pull into the town of Forbes to see our Aunty Frances and all her Mob. She's Uncle Paddy's first wife and her kids are Trish, who has polio, Gail and Billy. It's been a long drive already from the orange paddocks to Forbes so all of us are happy to get out and stretch our legs.

As soon as we get out of the car, we can tell something is dreadfully wrong because Aunty Frances runs to Mummy. She starts telling her some terrible news—that our house on the Island has burnt down while we were away working the fruits. Mummy's sitting there in the car, just looking shell-shocked. Rounding us kids up, she tells us to hurry up and get back in the car. We gotta go straight home and find out how bad it is.

It seems like forever, the rest of the drive to Condo. All the way, us kids don't say nothing. We just keep hoping it's not true. We can't believe it. It's just after Christmas; all our toys, our new clothes! My new doll's cradle—I never even played with it. Mummy put it on top of the wardrobe for when we came back home from doing the oranges—we can't take much with us picking. We only took our clothes and one favourite toy. I'm lucky I took my bride's doll.

This Christmas just gone, our Aunty June, Mummy's sister, came and gave us presents, too. We don't often see her. (I think Aunty June's rich 'cause she gives us pocket money). This year was our best Christmas yet but now we ain't got no house no more and we'll never play with our new toys again, ever.

We go straight to the Island. We go past my great aunt, Aunty Tilly

Goolagong's house where usually we'd stop and have a cup of tea. I turn around and look through the back of the car window to see if I can see my brothers and sister. They're hiding under the tarp that goes over the back of the ute.

I see Paddy put his head up, even though he's supposed to be hiding so the police don't see them in the back. I turn around and look at Mummy's face. She's biting her bottom lip and Daddy is clinging to the steering wheel; his knuckles are white to the bone. They're real worried. We drive down through the gutters and the kids stand up in the back of the ute now. We're all straining our necks to see where our house should be. Everyone's crying, even the boys. It's not fair. We just can't believe we got no house anymore.

All gone, there's nothing left, just ashes, soot, tin and dust where our house used to be. Mummy's head is down. I see her tears; they keep coming. She walks through the ashes, looking, kicking pieces of tin. Kicking bits and pieces of our burnt-out home around. I know she's looking for her photographs. Her photos, they're the most special thing to her in the world. Her heart is breaking alongside mine.

She finds our old tea canister that has the kangaroo and emu on it—the Bushell's tea tin. She stands over it and kicks it around with her foot, just a little. Then she picks it up, looks at it and throws it into the rest of the rubble. She heads back to the fire the boys have lit, and sitting on an old upside-down tin bucket, she looks deep into the flames.

Us kids, we don't know what to do. We all hurt deep down inside and none of us wants to be the first to cry again. Mummy makes the boys run and get our older brothers and sisters from where they live. She tells us we'll have to get a tent to live in for a while. We aren't too worried. We've done that heaps of times already.

Unloading the back of the ute, the big ones pitch the tent and us girls grab out food and cooking stuff ready to use. Mummy's cooking our dinner and the billy's on the boil. We always have a billy boiling so that a cup of tea can be had any time. We're cooking our tucker on the fire, too. We have stew and damper that first night which tastes real good.

We crawl into bed exhausted. Then us kids all start whispering to each other about our toys and new clothes and our favourite things that got burnt and we'll never see again.

Mummy tells us to go to sleep but I gotta go to the toilet up the back. It's made of scrap wood, tin and hessian bags, with a big deep hole and no roof on top. The hole has wood over it that's got a big circle in the middle to sit on. Sometimes, I get scared I might fall down the hole, it's so big. Lynnie has to take me. I giggle because I think it's funny that she has to get outta bed when she just got in. She pulls my hair and I pretend to scream, making out she hurt me, but I close my mouth just as quickly—we don't need no more upset for the day.

We walk past the fire. Mummy, she's just sitting doing nothing, just sitting there. We get to the toilet and I sit and dawdle, pulling my pants down real slow. I just don't wanna go to bed yet so I take longer than usual. Lynnie's yelling at me to hurry. Grabbing the newspaper, I rub it to make it soft before I wipe myself. Jumping off the toilet, I'm ready to go. I crawl back into bed and then I hear this crying.

'Lynnie, Mummy's crying,' I say. She tells me to shut up and go to sleep. I start crying, too, and so does she. The boys are quiet. I whisper to them but they won't answer; they're not making a sound. I bet they're crying, too.

***

We're camping in the tent now the house is gone. Uncle Paddy and Aunty Carol are off living somewhere else; they had been minding our house while we were away picking. Soon, my older brothers get some timber and tin and make a two-room hut for us to live in instead of living in the tent. One room is the kitchen and the other is our girls' room—the one that we gotta share with Mummy. Daddy's not around; he's gone to work again.

We've got just enough money to buy an old bus. The boys will sleep in there. My big sisters are gonna make curtains to pull across so it looks like there's a room; so they can have some privacy. The front of the bus is gonna be the family lounge room, with the boys' room up the back. They make it look good (not as good as our house, though—it was big and it was old). My bigger brothers and sisters don't live at home anymore but they still help when they gotta.

Mummy keeps the hut spotless; she's always so tidy. We aren't allowed to make too much of a mess and, if we do, we gotta clean it up. She's the best cook, too. She can make the best damper and stew you could ever eat. We have no stove yet so Mummy cooks on the outside fire, but she never burnt anything, anyway. We all don't mind living in the hut and in the bus. Mummy says, 'We're all still alive and that's what matters'. Sometimes, though, I miss living in a house. I miss my bed and my dolls.

We ain't got no electricity in our hut but Mummy's saving up so she can pay the council to put an electricity box in our yard. She has to save a lotta money. We live our life with fire and candles. It don't worry us too much;

we're used to it from the paddocks and when the river floods.

Finally, the council man is here. When he hooks our electricity box up, we have to pay one shilling (ten cents) for half an hour of electricity. We have to have lotsa coins. Soon, we have our very first television so we all sit in the lounge room in the bus watching it. Our very own TV! It's a PYE TV, only black and white, but we don't mind.

16

Too many tents, too much heartache

The paddocks call us back every year but some years are harder than the last. Images of tents, hard dirt and camping flood my mind as I try to sort out the jumble in my mind; living on hills and paddocks surrounded by family and cousins. Playing cricket and Lynnie being knocked out by the cricket ball and being rushed to the hospital. The sound of a baby girl crying, taking its last breath as we all sit inside our own tents knowing that the baby was going to heaven. The doctor had sent her back to us to be with her family when her time comes. Morning comes and sadness grips us all; my Uncle and Aunty prepare to take her back into town. Standing at the tent flap, I raise my eyes, looking for the sun, but no sunshine shows through on this day: it's cold and overcast. We don't go to work. We must be respectful to the dead.

One time, we're all camped out in tents again picking oranges; Uncle Paddy and Aunty Carol are here with us. Mummy's sick, real sick but I don't know exactly what it is. She has to have a big operation, I know that much. Uncle and Aunty are looking after us kids till she comes home and they're worried. One night, we're all out at the fire when Uncle Paddy tells us, 'Joyce's real sick in hospital; it don't look good. She might not come home.'

Paddy, Lynnie, Kevin and me are walking away from the fire broken-hearted. We crawl into our beds in our tent, praying that God will let her get better, that she comes home. We cry and whisper to each other, making sure nobody can hear us: 'What would we do without her? Who would take care of us?' We know already in our hearts that we'd be split up—we wouldn't be brothers and sisters anymore. And the fear of the Welfare grows deeper inside me every time I hear him mentioned.

Our greatest fear is not being brothers and sisters. Years later, I find out that, when our mother died, Aunty June wanted to take me and Uncle Raymond wanted to take Kevin but Mummy and Daddy wouldn't let them and so they took both of us themselves. And when Uncle Athol was alive, he begged Mummy that, if anything happened to him, she was to get his kids and take them. Mummy and Aunty Doris went and got Lynnie and Paddy from their mum and she didn't mind.

I say my prayers for Mummy to get better again, harder this time, praying that God in heaven makes her all right so she comes home to us. After a while in the hospital, she comes home and I say a thank you to God. I think maybe he might be all right after all.

17

What's a State Ward?

Lynnie and Paddy are darker than me and Kevin. People ask, 'How can you be sisters? She's white, you're black.' Lynnie tells them lots of reasons: 'She ate too much Vegemite when she was little' or 'Mummy left her in the oven too long'. But I love it best when she tells them, 'Mummy forgot to use the Persil'. We know from the ads on TV that Persil is the washing powder that 'makes everything white'. We walk away laughing. My big sister, she's so smart; I wanna be like her when I get bigger.

Other times, we trick people, too: the ones who don't know we're brothers and sisters. Like the man at the picture theatre with the little torch who tells you where to sit. Us four kids walk in. This is in the early 60s.

Shining his torch on Kevin and me, he says, 'You two sit there,' pointing to the chairs with the white people in them. Me and Kevin don't move. Us kids don't go nowhere without each other. Then he flashes it at Lynnie and Paddy and says, 'You two sit there down the front in the roped-off area where the Blackfellas sit'. We all say, at the same time, 'You can't do that, we're brothers and sisters'.

He looks at us all. I reckon he knows that there's no way he's gonna split us up so he sends us down to the front to where all our cousins are. We don't mind; we're happy down there. That's our family, too, and we're all together. We didn't wanna sit with them white people, anyway. And we would've got into big trouble with Mummy if we wouldn't have sat together, especially Paddy and Lynnie—their job is to look after us little ones.

***

Me, Kevin, Lynnie and Paddy, we're State Wards but I don't know what that means. I only know the awful fear that comes with those words. The fear that he could take me away from Mummy, take me away from my brothers and sisters; a fate worse than death. Lynnie says the Welfare's supposed to help us with our school clothes and stuff like that. I don't think that happened too often but he sent us to the dentist once to get our teeth checked.

I ask, 'What's State Wards mean?'

The other kids tell me it means, 'He's our boss, our legal guardian. He's our boss till we're all grown up, not Mummy. He tells Mummy what we can do or can't do.' I scream deep down inside then. Mummy's our boss, she tells us what to do. We don't need no Welfare man coming and telling us.

We all talk about him. 'He has no right telling Mummy what to do with us kids. We're happy; we're a good family.' Us four kids, Paddy, Lynnie, Kevin and me, make a pact that we'll all be good so the Welfare don't get no excuse to take us away. We make a promise to Mummy, even though she's not there.

'We'll be good, Mummy.'

Our Mummy would work her heart out for us kids to make sure that the Welfare wouldn't have an excuse to take us but I reckon if he tried, he would've had to kill her first. No way would she let anyone take us. No one was game even to smack us for being naughty; only she did that. Even Daddy's never allowed to hit us, not that he would, anyway.

I can't understand why anyone would want to take us away, but I have a dreadful fear in me like no other. Fear of the Welfare coming, fear of being sent to the homes ('cause that's where they send the bad kids or kids that the parents don't want or can't take care of). I promise myself I'll never be bad for the Welfare to take me or for Mummy not to want me. It's a horrible thing for any seven-year-old to be worrying about.

All of us are pretending we're brave and not scared but the terror strikes each one of us, right down deep inside our bellies. Anyway, we tell each other, 'If he tried to take us, we'd all die first before he got us'. Thoughts of mass suicide hits us like a brick in the face even if we didn't know what we're talking about.

I can see them coming to take me, trying to get me. I tell the other kids, 'I'd run and hide. They'd never find me.'

There's lots of hiding spots on the Island so, if they did find me, I wouldn't go. We all say the same thing, each one of us, thinking we're so tough and so smart.

'There's no way they're gonna take me and give me to someone else or put me in a home for bad kids.' I'm acting so tough as I mouth my words, but I feel my skin go clammy and cold. My face is quivering, my bottom lip trembles as I try not to let the tears come.

Then I remember sister, Meryl, telling the story of the time Mummy was really sick and had to go to hospital for a big operation. The doctors thought she was gonna die. She had no one to look after the six bigger kids—me and Kevin weren't born yet—so she had to tell the Welfare they were 'uncontrollable'. It was the only way she could get help to look after the big ones when she was in hospital, but they put my brother and sisters into a Home; I don't think Johnny and Darryl went. The place was in Sydney although I can't remember for sure. The people there did terrible things to my family, just terrible.

When they were kids in this home, Meryl had to make a bed on the floor beside Paddy's cot. This was so that she could change him and his sheets before the nuns came and found him wet in the morning. They used to flog him if he was. So, each morning before those bad people woke up, Meryl would change him and his cot sheets and then run back to her bed, pretending that she slept there all night and that everything was okay.

Mummy's never around when the older girls tell us these stories about the Home; she'd be upset to know what they had done to her kids. I hear the stories and I hate the Welfare so much. Soon, Mummy comes home and we're happy.

18

Cherry-picking time

We're still living on the Island in the humpy and the bus, and we keep heading for the work in the paddocks to earn a living and eventually to get another house. We do the cherries in Young and then head to Orange to start all over again. It's six o'clock in the morning. Mummy's singing out, 'Time to get up'. Okay, I don't want to get up, but I gotta. We gotta pick the cherries. If we don't, it's simple: no Christmas and no house.

There's Mummy getting our breakfast. She never complains unless the cherries are bad or green—then we can't earn as much money. My brothers are yawning and pulling the blankets over their heads and Lynnie's still pretending to be asleep. Me, I just don't wanna get up *at all.*

Mummy's hurrying us, telling us to move. I hold my breath hoping she'll let me stay asleep. I pull the blanket around me tighter, telling Mummy I'm tired and feeling sick, too; trying just a bit harder to escape getting out of bed this early in the morning. It's freezing cold out there where the fruit is.

She tells me that the fire is going outside so I'm to get out of bed in ten minutes. When I'm feeling better, then I have to come down to the paddock and work. Mummy didn't like leaving us anywhere by ourselves for too long; she always worried about us. Me, I'm happy. I knew I could do it, get away with blue murder. The other kids are calling me a sook.

I don't care. I lie back, counting my blessings—how happy I am—but then I think about the cherries and how we're supposed to work really hard. Slowly, I climb out of bed and get dressed and head down to the cherry trees. My feet are dragging. I kick the dirt, dust flying all around, my heart aching as tears run down my face in the cold. I look around at the cherry trees. I reckon we would've picked every single one in all the years that our families been coming here.

It's the same when we go to Young, too; we pick all the time at Cunich's. Gegg, he's our boss; he thinks the world of Mummy and us kids. He saves our job for us every year and our hut, too. Every year, we come back to the same bosses and the same paddocks. I tell everyone I was born under a cherry tree 'cause it sure feels like it. I meet Lynnie halfway because Mummy sent her back to come get me.

Matt, our boss in Orange, is pretty good, too, and he saves our hut for us each picking season. It isn't really a hut, it's actually an old rundown railway carriage and cold. It feels like the morning air finds its way through every little crack in the walls just so it can make us colder. It's divided into two rooms, one for us girls and Mummy, and the front room for the boys and the tucker.

There's no kitchen, just a dish and a tea towel that gets used every tucker time and gets cleaned and put away after every meal. We make our furniture out of old boxes and old picking tins. Mummy puts tablecloths and tea towels over everything to make it look nice.

It's home for the next couple of weeks so we gotta make the best of it. The old train has lotsa holes in it. Us kids gotta screw up and wet old newspaper to plug them up; we make a game of it, even though it's so freezing.

Another day and I hear Mummy's voice again. 'It's up and at 'em'—her favourite saying—'Cherry-picking time.' I drag my poor little body out of that warm bed. 'It's cold, Mummy.' She puts another log on the fire outside, building it up so it hasn't died out by the time we get out there. We'll warm ourselves up before walking to the row we are working on. I rub my eyes and try to make my body move.

Time to head down to the paddock. At Matt's place, you don't have too far to get to your rows and it's easy to carry your buckets and your ladders from tree to tree and row to row. Matt gives each family a certain number of rows so that we'll get big trees and little trees, good trees and bad trees. It's also a way for him to keep a check on how you treat the trees and who are the good pickers.

In some other paddocks, it seems like you gotta walk for miles or sometimes, if the cherry trees are too far away, the boss will pick you up on the tractor. Then, you gotta load your buckets and your ladders on, too. Sometimes, the other pickers, they'll take your favourite bucket or ladder and, when they do, it causes us more work. It's easy to get angry with them when you gotta walk all around the paddock and find it and lug it back. Picking can be really hard work and we have to work harder than the white people, too. They get more money for a pound of cherries than we do. We only get ten cents a pound while they get twenty cents. It doesn't seem fair to me, even as a little kid, especially since we're the hardest workers Matt's got. One day, I ask Mummy why we get paid less than white people. She tells me, 'That's the way it is'.

Although we get paid less, Matt is pretty good. He looks after us and treats Mummy with respect and is kind to us kids. After the cherries are over, he lets us stay and get all the leftover fruit, like the ones that didn't ripen in time, so we can earn extra money. It's not too bad but it's harder to pick a lot as the trees may only have a handful left on them. We have to lug our heavy ladder to a tree but might only get ten cherries off it and then have to lug it again to the next. Us kids have fun in the paddock by ourselves, though, and we don't work too hard once the season is ending. I think we play more than we pick. Our poor old Mummy—she always works hard.

Once we have picked all the leftover cherries, we sell them door-to-door, trying to earn that extra dollar. People are pretty good, too. The ones we sell to, they usually buy them. We make sure there's no kids around when we sell door-to-door as we really don't like being teased for doing it. We don't mind too much here in Orange, though, 'cause we don't know anybody in this town.

Mummy, she's a 'gun' picker, even in Young. That means she's the best picker in the paddock but she also picks a lot of buds. Me and Mummy, we've got a trick that Matt or Gegg don't know about. When you pick cherries, you're not allowed to pick the buds—they're the leaves with the new buds on them—because that's next year's fruit. The very first job you get as a tiny kid is to pick the buds out of the cherry box and hide them. This is my job from when I'm old enough to know what a bud is. I get them from the bin every time Mummy empties her buckets so that they don't find them in amongst the cherries.

But the best job is to run around the tree and pick up all the buds that have fallen on the ground, and then run and hide them. Sometimes, I dig a little hole in the dirt and bury them or I'll climb up another tree, real high, and hide them in the fork. I always have to hurry and to be real careful that Matt or Gegg don't catch me or find all of the buds. I don't want Mummy to get into trouble. These cherries are our ticket to a new life, a house and escaping the Welfare.

19

All the way to Grafton Jail

It's 1967 and all those whispers about another father were true!

Lynnie wasn't lying; she was telling the truth. Another father and he's me and Kevin's, not Lynnie's or Paddy's or anyone else's but ours. He belongs to nobody but us two. Mummy tells us we're going to see him. She must think me and Kevin's real grown-up now. I'm still seven so I must be big enough to know about grownup things. Feeling special, deep down inside me I glow, feeling love in my heart for this man and knowing, too, that somebody else loves me.

We're gonna go and see our Dad in Grafton Jail. Grafton is a long, long way away and Daddy is gonna drive us there.

'What time we going, Mummy?' I ask.

'Sparrow fart.'

So I know we're going before the birds wake up. We're excited because it's our first trip without the other kids which makes us feel important and grown-up at the same time.

Kevin and me are on our best behaviour; we don't want nothing to stop us from seeing our Dad. We play games to make the time go faster: spot the milepost, spot the number plates starting with 'S' or maybe 'H', make words from them. Then it's 'I spy with my little eye something that starts with T'—it has to be in the car: thermos! Mummy has tea and sandwiches for us to eat along the way. We laugh a lot, excited. Mummy sings her favourite songs to us, then we sing with her. Daddy keeps driving. The miles from Condo go fast; we're getting closer to him with each minute.

Mummy starts crying for her baby brother. She tells us, again, about being good—no crying—and what it might be like when we see him. Daddy tries to stop her from being sad, saying, 'It's all right, Joyce. It's all right.' Kevin and me stop smiling. We look at each other, sit back and don't say nothing for a long time. No more games. I feel like crying, too.

There's Grafton. It's got lots of funny trees growing everywhere. We ask Mummy what they are. She tells us they're banana trees, but there's no paddocks. Me and Kevin can't believe it; the fruit trees are everywhere.

We have a little holiday in town and stay in our first motel, ever; I think I'm a real lady, pretending to be real flash with lotsa money, living like kings and queens. We can even run out and pick a banana off the tree but we gotta be careful to get a ripe one. Me and my brother get on so good, not fighting or mucking up, and I know that Mummy and Daddy are real proud of us.

Tomorrow, we're gonna see our Dad.

20

Behind the bars

This is our first time meeting him, this man who is our Dad, but I know nothing about him. My real father—that sounds so good—I like the way it rolls off my tongue: 'my real father'. There's a sweetness to the words that I never felt before but that doesn't mean I don't love Daddy. I do—he's my father—but now I've got two fathers; that's something so special and so good.

I'm excited. I don't have to share him with anyone, only Kevin. Having two fathers made me different from the other kids. Having another father made me different 'cause when you're the baby of eight you get lost in everyone else's world. I'm sad for Lynnie and Paddy, though; their real Dad (Uncle Athol) died but ours didn't—only our mother (Goma). At least we all still got Mummy and Daddy to share.

Telling us about what it will be like seeing him, Mummy tries to tell us that he will be in a big place where they keep people. It might be scary. We don't understand but say, 'Yes, Mummy'. She says that we have to be good, that we can't cry when we leave or in front of him and to make sure to tell him that we love him.

Mummy never cries but she's crying. She's saying, 'It might be hard for us—we might not be able to touch him or talk to him much'. She doesn't tell us why. She wouldn't have told us or let any of my older brothers or sisters tell us; it was her way of protecting us. That's why Lynnie would've got a hiding if she did tell why she made me promise not to say nothing.

We're there at last and we go into the jail. It *is* scary. Big redbrick walls and barbed wire loom in front of me. Walking down a long hall, the walls feel like they are crashing into me. There's nothing but brick and iron bars. This place is so gigantic. Clutching Mummy's hand, I cling tighter with each step we take. I want to hide behind her skirt and never let go.

We walk for a while and there's a wooden seat plank stuck out from the wall. Above it, there's a square window with bars across it. The man in uniform tells Mummy to wait before he goes away and comes back out. She looks through the window and talks to someone. She stands Kevin up on the seat to see him. Then it's my turn now.

On tiptoes, I try to stretch my body as far as I can so he can see me. He's behind the brick wall and the window's real small, just a square cut into the wall. The bars are so thick; we want to force our face between them but we can't.

We take it in turns, me and Kevin, standing up there. He makes us turn our faces this way and that so he can see what we look like. We aren't allowed to touch him or to put our hands up to his face and he can't touch us neither. He tells us to walk right back to the other side of the hall so he can see how grown-up we are. I walk back to the other side and turn this way and that way so that he can see how grown-up his two babies are. He tells us how handsome Kevin is and how pretty I am. My belly does flip-flops; I'm beaming from deep down inside with happiness.

We're smiling. Love is all over us from loving this man with the sad eyes staring at us from behind the bars in a wall. We visit and talk. Mummy's turn again. She tells him how the rest of the family are going, how the house got burnt down and everything else she thinks he needs to know; hiding her tears behind her hanky.

The man in uniform comes over and says we gotta leave. We start walking out but then we both turn at the same time and yell, 'We love you'. The hall reveals itself in front of us again. An eternity flashes past us before we reach the outside. Sadness is deep inside me with a hundred million questions.

> How come he's there, Mummy?
> When is he coming home, Mummy?
> How come there's all that barbed wire around the place?
> Why couldn't we see him again, Mummy?
> Why couldn't we touch him, Mummy?

We ask those questions, getting some answers but not. Some things are better off left unsaid. I look at Mummy's face and glimpse the tears that well from deep inside her heart. Her eyes are so sad; sad like my father's eyes were. My brother has his head down, lost in his own thoughts, like me. He's not knowing what to do. Maybe he's feeling like me; he don't know what to say, just feeling helpless, a feeling like you're drowning in the river and no one's reaching out to save you.

I wonder why life has to be so bad to us that it wants to cause us all this misery. Our house burns down, my father's locked in a bad place and I don't know why. Mummy's sad, our father's sad, today me and Kevin are sad, too. And we got the Welfare.

We go home to the other kids and tell them all about our visit. I start crying as I tell Lynnie. Me and Kevin don't talk too much about it. I guess we really don't understand what's going on. All the grown-ups in the family want to hear the news and want to know how our father is doing. They come for a visit: Uncle Paddy, Aunty Carol, everyone. All us kids are sent outside to play. We know we're not allowed to be around when the grown-ups are talking. 'Kids are seen and not heard.'

I hear Daddy and Uncle Paddy telling Mummy that everything will be all right and not to cry. 'He'll be home one day, Joyce.' I wanna run away and hide; I hate it when she cries.

In a few days, she yells out to Kevin and me to show us a letter and photos she is sending to Dad. On the back of the photo she wrote, 'To Dad, love Kerry xx' or 'To Dad, love Kevin xx'. We know now we have this Dad—one that's locked away and miles from us. Today, she has a parcel to send to him. Soon, however, memories of our father get lost in everyday life.

21

Earning a quid

Uncle Paddy comes and takes us rabbiting. He loves hunting and we love going with him. We come back with the best mob of rabbits you ever did see. Uncle lets us pick good ones to give to Mummy. I guess he thought they'd cheer her up. Usually, he keeps the good ones and sells them.

I'm about eight when brother Johnny, and his wife, Beryl, come to live with us in the bus. The bigger boys add another room onto the hut for Paddy and Kevin. One day, Nay is screaming. He fell on his bottle and cut his face bad. There's blood everywhere. They rush him to the hospital and he has to have stitches down his cheek; it doesn't look good.

Nay, he likes to have black tea in his bottle with a little bit of sugar—it's his favourite. But the people at the hospital, they don't like him having black tea and sugar in his bottle. Beryl says that it's the only way he goes to sleep.

Us kids visit him on the ward and, when they're not looking, we run and make him a bottle just the way he likes it. The hospital's old and scary, too; we gotta walk a long way to go and see him 'cause where they have him is right at the back. They kept Aboriginal people in a different ward: one for them and one for us. Nay comes home from hospital and the wound heals. It leaves a scar but he looks as cute as he did before.

We go back to school and Mummy looks for whatever work she can find. She gets a job as a cook at a pub. Sometimes, when we have enough money to buy a lolly at Archie's fish-and-chip shop, we go up there from school during lunchtime, to say hello to her.

At the shops, we might get an old sixpence in our change and, if we do, we save it and take it home to Mummy because she likes to save old coins. Us kids love it when that happens; that means we're doing something special for her, for once—she's always doing something special for us.

Sometimes, Mummy would give us spending money on the way to school. We stop at Wright Heaton's, our favourite shop, and buy sixpence worth of hard-boiled lollies or a shilling's-worth of broken biscuits. Mr Wright Heaton, he gives us good biscuits as well as the broken ones, and I always seem to get more than the other kids, the lollies, too. If we only have a sixpence or a shilling for the lot of us, the other kids send me into the shop to get the biscuits or lollies. Mr Wright Heaton always gives me a big bagful, even bigger than before.

***

We earn our pay whichever way we can. Mummy usually gets work up town or out in the bush stick-picking or felling trees. She can work as hard as any man, if not better. Other times, to earn a quid, we do different things like going resin hunting or copper-wire hunting. We mainly do that if Daddy's home or if someone can drive us to places to look for it 'cause we need a car to take us out in the bush. All Mummy's money is spent on feeding and clothing us kids. That's the most important thing to her. We always gotta have a feed in our bellies and a roof over our heads.

Today, we're going resin hunting: to get the sap from the gum trees. We go out along the road, then we head off on foot into the bush so that we can find lots of it. Us kids split up in all different directions but the rule is, we always gotta stay within cooee of each other, otherwise we'd get lost. But Mummy always said, 'If you got lost in the bush at night, you only gotta follow the evening star and that will lead you home'.

Us kids are armed with a tin and knife. We scrape the resin from the tree and put into our tin so that Mummy can sell it to the chemist. He makes medicine from it. Today, we're really lucky: the trees have lots to give and we gotta get a lot, otherwise we don't get much money.

We love being out in the scrub because we can play and look out for goannas and blue-tongue lizards, too.

When we get close to the goannas, they run up the trees away from us but we follow and check them out—they can be really big. Watching their powerful bodies making their way up into a tree is a beautiful sight indeed, and some are so big. I reckon I seen one that was nearly as big as Daddy, and that's big.

Kevin nearly gets bitten by a blue-tongue lizard one day. He was tormenting him, poking a stick at him; the blue-tongue was getting angry and sticking his frill neck out at Kevin and hissing. He's lucky Mummy didn't catch him. She would've been angry at him for teasing the lizard; she won't let any of us be cruel to animals (not that we would be). She says that this is where they live and we have to be respectful of that.

When we're out in the bush, we gotta keep our eyes out for snakes, too. Mummy makes us wear our school shoes out here; if we got bit by a King Brown or a red-bellied black, we'd know it for sure. We're lucky when we come out here in the bush: it seems all the animals and even the birds want to put on a parade for us. Above us, we hear the cockatoos screeching their messages to the world and we watch the galahs playing and preening. Sometimes, we just lie on the ground and watch them all fly over, thankful for the wonderful land we belong to and for the gift of nature—life, birds, trees and us.

It's wonderful to be here in the scrub. The leaves rustle with the wind and the gum trees reach right up to the sky. Sometimes, I am that goanna, climbing the tree right up to the top where it meets the blue of the heavens.

It's the same when we go copper-wire hunting. We go out in the scrub and anywhere else that people have dumped old cars and rubbish, looking for the wire and old batteries. We even find some on the side of the road where someone's car has broken down. We make sure that we grab every little piece; it all adds up to get money for us. Even if we find any little bits as we're walking up the street or anywhere, we put them in our pocket and bring them home.

We earn most of our money doing the fruits. We've always gone to pick the cherries in Young and Orange but we do the other fruits, too, like the oranges in Leeton and the grapes in Griffith. Usually, we do most of our fruit-picking during the school holidays but now that the house is burnt down, we gotta travel more to pick whatever fruit's in season.

Things have changed, though. When we're out in the paddocks now, us kids go to school during the week and do picking on the weekend. Sometimes, if it's not too late or dark, we'll pick more fruit in the afternoons after doing our homework. Not having a proper house means Mummy's working harder than ever before. It's real important to keep us fed and housed but even more so now: living in the hut and the bus is a big problem—the Welfare man told Mummy we gotta have a house in six months' time or else he's taking us kids away. But he never gave us no help in getting one!

When he told Mummy that, she called a family conference. She told us four kids that we would have to go picking a lot more so we could stay together. We need to live in Leeton, not just visit when we picked. Us kids, small as we were, were determined to do what needed to be done to keep the family together. We knew the importance of being together, and the fear of the Welfare was always in our minds.

***

The terror of the Welfare splitting us up is the biggest problem in my life but the Welfare man isn't the only problem. In one place we were living in, big sister Maureen is living with her husband, Sam.

One day, I gotta go somewhere with Sam and I don't wanna go. I have to sit in the front seat of the car, next to him. Maureen is standing on the lawn, the white house in the background behind her, and one of the boys on her hip as we're leaving. I watch my sister from out of the passenger-door window, my face and hands clinging to the glass, hoping she can tell I don't wanna go with him. She watches us drive away.

He takes me to a building and we go around the back under the floor boards—it's built high in the air on stilts. He pulls my pants down and says, 'I'll tell Joyce and she'll send you away, and the Welfare will come and get you'.

Afterwards, he takes me back home. I don't say nothing to anyone but I hurt and I feel funny. Me and Lynnie are always scared to be alone with him, but no one can save us, not even Mummy, 'cause he'll tell them we were bad and the Welfare will come and take us away.

22

The school's racist

We're going to do the prunes at a little place outside of Young. It's just Mummy and us four kids. Picking prunes isn't so bad. You gotta shake the tree to knock all the plums down to pick them up from the ground and fill your case that way. There's a big shed here on the Boss's property where they take the plums and dry them out, then make them into prunes. The boss is pretty good here and there's not many other pickers.

You name it, we can pick it. We're all good pickers, even Paddy, although we reckon he eats more than he picks, sometimes. As seasoned pickers, we pack our stuff up and go onto another paddock, another fruit. Even though we work so hard, especially Mummy, we all have fun telling jokes and laughing real loud. I love it best when we have smoko and have a spell from the picking, sitting under the tree having a good yarn. Mummy always brings us good food to eat, too.

Mummy sends us to the primary school that's located in the town. It's a little one, kindergarten to sixth class, and only one teacher who's also the principal. But we don't go to class all the time. One day, the principal tells us four kids to sit on the front verandah instead of being in class. We're happy, the other kids—the white kids—they gotta stay indoors and do schoolwork but we don't have to.

We just sit outside and do nothing; we're so lucky and we're even luckier still because we don't have to pick prunes till the weekend. It's kinda fun; it feels like we're having a bit of a holiday! But it sure can get boring. We don't tell Mummy about the principal not letting us into his classroom with everyone else. She would go after him, wanting to know why. After a while, we tell Mummy we don't wanna go to school; we wanna help her pick 'cause getting a house is more important. In our hearts, we knew that was never gonna work though because, no matter what the Welfare demanded, we have to go to school wherever we are. Finally, we finish the prunes and head back to Condo again.

The families are excited we're home again and Meryl asks us what the paddocks were like. We tell her about the principal and how we sat outside most of the time. She's pretty angry and yells out to Mummy, telling her what the principal did, that he didn't want us at his school. Mummy's real upset and swears we will never go to that school again. Years later, we go back to doing the prunes but we never went back to the school.

23

Decimal currency in Sydney

In 1966, we move to Sydney for work, near Granville where Uncle Raymond lives. Our new house; it's big and bright and has plenty of room for us to play. It's Easter time and so Mummy puts all our Easter eggs beside our beds for us to wake up and find. During the night, our dog, Blue, came along and ate each and every one! He's old and spoilt so nobody really goes crook on him. We laugh and call him a pig—we hope he gets a bellyache.

I'm nine and in class 3A at Punchbowl Primary School. Lynnie's gone to a different school over in Bankstown. I miss having her around but I love my new school and the kids. I play elastics and I'm really good at it. Punchbowl's a good school and the teachers are nice; I'm happy I'm in 3A.

Mummy is working in a factory and she gets our grown-up step-cousin,

Sandra, to look after us. But Sandra's mean and does really bad things, too. She makes us stand against the wall all the time. We have to stand with our hands above our head and our elbows touching the wall, and we're not allowed to move an inch. She tells us, 'Aunty Joyce will send you away. You'll go to the homes. I'll tell her you was bad and the Welfare will come and get you.'

The Welfare.

My skin crawls when I hear that word and I feel my belly tie itself up in knots. I hate the Welfare man. I hate him more than anything in the world. I've got this fire burning inside me with all my hate for him. If he couldn't take me away, things would be different. I could tell Mummy what's happening and she wouldn't let me get in the car with Sam anymore and she wouldn't let Sandra look after us kids, neither. But I can't tell her 'cause they said they would tell Mummy I was *bad* and she would send me away. Bad girls go to the homes with the Welfare man. They said Mummy don't love bad girls.

***

It's hard in Sydney being all at different schools. Us Condo kids don't belong here. The kids at Paddy's school pick on him, especially. Each afternoon, we all wait for each other and, nearly every day, a gang of boys will be chasing Paddy, wanting to belt him. Lynnie stands beside him ready to fight them. Kevin and me have rocks in our hands, ready in case they decide to attack us all. We stand together after school threatening them to come a little bit closer but they never do. We turn around and walk away, laughing, calling them chickens. They call us names like Abos, boongs, coons and niggers.

On the weekend, my cousins come over and we play football together. My cousin Joe, he plays in a football team so we gotta help him train. I'm a tomboy and I love footy nearly as much as I love fishing. I go to catch the ball and slip in a hole; I twist my ankle but I don't say nothing 'cause the others would tease me. When it's Monday morning, I can't put my school shoe on so I've gotta tell Mummy. She takes me to the doctors at a big hospital and they wrap my leg up in sticky tape plaster, right up to the knee. The doctor gives me a lollipop and sends me home.

It seems we just don't belong in Sydney: Kevin gets hit by a car and is in hospital with a bandage around his head. Mummy's really worried. We go up to the hospital to see him and are thankful that he's not too bad. We tease him about getting outta school—trying to make him laugh, make him feel better. Soon he comes home and Mummy tells us to look after him to make sure he's all right.

Now I hate Sydney and I wanna go back to the Island, even if our house isn't there. I wanna feel the dirt between my toes. I wanna play 'pick up sticks' and 'Simon says' out on the road, and I wanna see if our spirit is still there. I wanna go back to the Island so bad I feel myself bursting inside, right down to my belly button from wanting it so bad. I wanna go home and be happy.

I guess, looking back now, Mummy knew we just ain't city people and needed to go home where we belonged. And we all missed our Condo family so much. Sydney's just too far away from everyone; and my two big sisters and Beryl were all gonna have babies so we had to be home for that. After about eight months in Sydney, we packed up and headed home to a house in Condo in Orange Lane, just across from Meryl's. It's not the Island but at least we're back in our old hometown.

***

We're back. We run and kiss everyone, excited to be where we belong. All the family come over for a big feed and to find out how Sydney went. Hooray! We're home; we belong in the bush. I think about the things we used to do on the Island. I remember my big sisters when they wore their long dresses, with petticoats everywhere, singing their songs. I start to sing.

'Some day, I'm gonna write the story of my life...'

I feel better already.

Maureen has another baby boy, Steven, and Beryl and Johnny are expecting one, too, and so is Meryl. It's August: Beryl's in hospital and the Condo Show is on again. We all go to the Show dressed up in our pretty dresses and the boys looking real good in their shorts and pants.

We have lotsa fun at the Show and, after we've spent all our money, it's time to go home. We're loaded up with Tiki dolls and stuffed toys. Paddy and Kevin are real good at winning things—sometimes, Paddy gives his prizes to us as well. Now and again, they'll distract the man and put the hooks on the stand when he's not looking. We saved enough money to call the hospital from the public phone, and when Lynnie rings, they tell her Beryl's had a baby girl, but we're not allowed to go to the hospital—they say no kids are allowed. So we save up all the things we won at the show and wait for the baby niece to come home. They call her Narelle.

In October 1966, I turn ten and, in December, Meryl has another baby girl called Jasmine. Now we've got three handsome nephews and two beautiful nieces.

Daddy comes back from the railways and is living with us again. It's good to have him around but he's real strict, making me and Lynnie have our school uniform only six inches above the knee, just as the school rules say. He makes us sit on the floor on our knees and Mummy has to use the ruler to make sure it's a perfect six inches. We're real cheeky kids. As soon as we're out of sight of home, we hitch that uniform a little bit higher. Daddy soon has to head off back to work again. We miss him but it's pretty good, too, when there's only us four kids and Mummy together.

It's great being home at Condo, even if we ain't on the Island. We go and visit over there but it's not the same since our house burnt down. All we have now are our memories of playing in that red dirt and all the fun things we used to do. We're back at school and everything is good. We still go and do the fruits when they come on but now it's mainly over the school holidays and Christmas as we can't really miss too much school. Mummy still always has to look over her shoulder in case of the Welfare; she can never relax.

24

Back to the paddocks

It's time to head back to the paddocks; this time, it's over to Leeton to pick the oranges. The paddocks are hard work but we tell jokes and sing songs, too, and have a little play around. We really work hard. Mummy works the hardest—even harder than Daddy. He's not with us again on this trip.

Sometimes, it's real hot and all you wanna do is sit in the shade of the tree and do nothing. But we know we gotta make a living. Some of the trees are really big and have lotsa fruit on them. Mummy always tries to give us kids the side with the shade, when she can, but no matter how you try to fit your body into the shade of the tree, the sun always seems to find you. Mummy's always standing on a ladder, picking the fruit off the top of the tree. It's the hardest job. The bigger kids pick the sides of the tree—that way, it's easier for them to reach the fruit. And me,

I'm the smallest, so I gotta crawl into the middle of the tree to get all the ones inside. That's my job and I'm pretty good at it; I never leave any behind.

Oranges are fun but you gotta watch the spikes on the branches; you can get lotsa scratches if you're not careful. So we all wear long-sleeved shirts, even if it's boiling hot, and we even wear gloves 'cause the thorns scratch you to bits. Mummy always wears a floppy old canvas hat and an old man's long-sleeved flannelette shirt, otherwise she'd be burnt real bad. She tries to make us kids wear a hat, too. Each morning, as we leave the hut, our hats are on our heads but they don't last there too long.

When I'm climbing in the middle of the trees, I really do like feeling important helping my family although I always worry a little bit about scratching my face. Some days, when it's really hot and the sweat is dripping off you and your body is all sticky and wet, you really don't feel like picking. Then, Mummy will give us lotsa spells. In the morning and afternoon, when it's time for a spell, Mummy sings out 'smoko'. Quick as lightning, we flick our buckets from around our necks and sit in the shade. We all know we can sit and rest for twenty minutes. Us kids tease Mummy. We ask her if we can have a smoke, too, since it's called 'smoko' and she has one. She laughs with us and tells us 'no' and she hopes we never pick up 'the dirty things'.

Mummy has a cup of tea and us kids get a cold drink from the water bottle. We got two: one filled up with water and the other with cordial. It's just what you need to cool down and we always have something to eat, too—biscuits or cakes. We have little spells, too, but we gotta wait for smoko for a big spell.

When it's lunchtime, Mummy sings out, 'Tuckertime!' Then we have lunch underneath the tree that we just finished picking. We got a tucker bag filled with bread and butter, Vegemite, tomatoes and onions and even a can of baked beans. If the paddock is close to our hut, Mummy will send us girls down to turn the jug on and to start making sandwiches for everyone but that doesn't happen too often because, most times, the paddocks are too far away.

Picking fruit comes in pretty handy, too, if you've done something wrong, because Mummy can't get to you to give you a smack. She'll just tell you off; but sometimes, if you did something that's real bad, she'll wait till smoko and get you then. Usually, her telling you off is good enough. I think all our energy, especially Mummy's, is taken up picking the fruit and climbing the ladders so she never worries too much on wasting her energy trying to catch us.

If we've done something wrong and the Boss has caught us, we had better tell Mummy before he does, so we wait until Mummy's around the other side of the tree and sing out to her then. When she answers, we start to tell her.

'Mummy.'

'Yes, babe.' I can tell in her voice she's tired.

'You know we weren't supposed to go swimming in the dam yesterday after we knocked off?'

'Yes, babe.'

'Well, it was real hot so we thought we'd have a swim to cool off and the Boss caught us.'

Then she'll start telling us off. We gotta tell her, though. We'd be in a lot more trouble if the Boss told her before we did.

Each day, we gotta pick enough cases or bins to get enough money to keep us and get a house. Every morning, Mummy tells us how many cases or bins we need for the day and, when we get that many, then we can knock off. We always gotta fill our quota for the day. Usually, Mummy stays in the paddocks a bit longer.

25

Blue, the 'hero' dog

We head back and forth from Condo to the paddocks, always travelling to where the fruit-picking work is. When we get home, we live in rented places. Now that we no longer got our place on the Island, we gotta live up the street in town, surrounded by tar and cement and streetlights and buildings and people. Very different to how we used to live on the Island. We survive in town until it's time to go working the next time. We're heading back to pick the oranges in Leeton again, where we live in a hut on the Boss's paddock. It's much easier when that happens. He just takes our rent out of Mummy's pay. I'm still the smallest. I still gotta climb under the branches and get into the middle so I can pick the oranges that can't be reached from the outside.

I have fun in there. If I can see Mummy isn't looking, I can chuck an orange at the other kids but picking oranges can be hard work and we don't have cases no more. The Boss has got these things called crates that hook to the back of the tractor. Our crates are pretty big so it takes a while to fill them. In some paddocks, they gotta a cage on the back of the tractor and we gotta fill them instead.

Now we don't have smoko but we have the radio playing music to listen to and we still laugh a lot and tell jokes. We tell funny little stories about each other like, 'Remember last year when we was picking the cherries at Matt's and Paddy did this' or 'What about when we was at Gegg's and Kerry did that'.

Maureen's with us this time. She's still in love with Sam but I think they had a fight. We sing her favourite song for her: 'Sad Movies'. We sing lotsa other ones, too, trying to cheer her up. She smiles up at us but I think her heart is breaking.

Each afternoon, after we finish picking, we play for a while and then we sit out in the dirt and sing all the songs that we heard on the wireless. I'm a little bit sick one day and don't go picking. Mummy comes down from the paddock to check on me and to get lunch ready. She don't like leaving us anywhere by ourselves for too long—she always worries. She shows me a suitcase full of brand-new clothes for me and Kevin. There's a real pretty dress in there. Mummy says I can wear it to the Condo Show next year. There's no clothes for Lynnie and Paddy, though. I ask her why and she surprises me when she says, 'It's from your Nanna and Pop and they live in Gulgong'.

I never knew we had them as well! I have grandparents and I don't even know 'em. I think it's not fair though that Lynnie and Paddy don't get nothing. Mummy says she'll buy them something on pay day, so until then, she'll put the new things under the bed so no one knows.

It's Sunday, our day off. Mummy's cleaning up again. She's already cleaned our hut and now she's sweeping the dirt outside. Lynnie, Kevin and me are playing marbles in the dirt, playing quiet for a change. We look up now and again to see what she's doing.

Mummy sweeps all the dirt and rubbish in a bundle and finds a match and lights it. I'm waiting for her to tell me I can sprinkle the dirt with the water again. We hear a noise and look up from our marbles and scream, 'Fire! Mummy, the hut's on fire!'

Mummy makes sure all us kids are okay and hustled away from the fire but we can't find Maureen. She's in the hut, sleeping. Blue, the dog, goes in barking, trying to get her but he keeps running in and out. When he comes out, we tell him to get Maureen; we can't see her coming. Mummy tries to go in after her but she can't—the flames are too fierce.

We watch the door, panicking, but then, all of a sudden, we see her crawling out on her hands and knees. Blue wasn't leaving her behind; he was just going back in and checking to make sure she was coming behind him. Outside, Maureen tells us how he was waking her up by dragging her off the bed by the hair—he's so clever. We love him even better now that he saved our big sister. Blue's our hero. We laugh about how he got his practice pulling us kids out of the river.

There's no real loss to the Boss 'cause they just chuck anything together for us to live in. Our hut was just four walls and a roof made from lots of old wood, and a dirt floor. I reckon it looked like the hut made by the little pig in the nursery rhyme: anyone could've huffed and puffed, and it would've all fallen down, anyway.

We've got no clothes, no tucker, no nothing. Even the new clothes hidden under the bed burnt, too, but I really don't mind. Mummy makes sure we don't go without a feed. No fire would make her kids go without, and anyway, she puts all the money down her chest so we know there's some there for when we need it.

**

We ask how the fire started. There had been a big bang; the big boys must've left a live bullet lying around from when they went rabbiting and Mummy must have swept it up with the dirt and rubbish. It exploded when she lit the fire and the sparks went onto the hut. So now, with no hut, we're back living in a tent again. When the oranges finish, it's time to go home to Condo. Once again, we are living with all our family around us beside the Lachlan River which is such a big part of our lives. My Great Aunty, Tilly Goolagong, is the best fisherwoman in Condo; we all go fishing with her. She makes us walk for miles around the riverbank to get to her most favourite spots. We all love fishing and we're all good at it, except I don't like gutting them and seeing all their insides coming out so my job is to scale them instead.

I don't mind this job because I watch the pretty colours on the scales from the sun. I get them all over me and that means it's time for a swim. But we're not allowed to swim where the lines are and disturb the fish, so after all that long walk to the fishing spot, we gotta walk up the bank some more. Us kids can walk for miles, though. It's all part of bush living.

26

Christmas under the cherry tree

It's still 1965 and we're still working for our house. It's time again for the cherries. We all work real hard on the cherries, and this year, we can't go home for Christmas. We can't afford it 'cause we gotta get this house so we'll stay here in the paddocks. But that's okay—we've had Christmas here before. When its knock-off time, Mummy sends us back to the hut and us kids go and wash up and tidy up, then we play for a while. Hide'n-go-seek is great here; there's lots of room and trees to hide in. All the while, Mummy keeps working longer hours than anyone.

We take it in turns doing the chores here, too. The boys have to peel the potatoes for tea, and Lynnie and me have to get the wood in. I can cut the bigger wood now—not the big logs yet—but I'm real proud of myself, anyway. Mummy comes home when it's getting dark. We're all tired so she's cooking while we have our showers. Two more days to payday, then we can do our Christmas shopping. Santa comes in five days.

Just before payday comes, Mummy tells us how much money we'll have. She tallies up how much we have picked and earned each day, and how much we need for the house. She says we'll have four dollars and fifty cents each for our presents. She's sorry but that's all we can have to buy our presents from Santa. We say it's okay; we don't mind. She asks us what we would like Santa to bring. I don't know, maybe a doll. She says, 'On pay day, you can spend the afternoon in town and look around to see what you want. And you'll all have your own pocket money, too, so you can buy presents for each other.'

Pay day is finally here. We work real hard in the morning so we can have the afternoon off. Mummy tells us to take it easy, not to worry too much, that we'll be fine. We all feel happy—we can go into town and spend up big, well, pretend anyway. Mummy makes sure we're all dressed in our best clothes and that our faces are clean. No way would she let us go to town looking untidy or dirty.

When we go in, we have a special lunch at the café and then we're allowed to go and spend our pay on what we want, as long as it's not heaps of lollies. The boys would love to spend all their money on them. Last week, I bought some paper dolls that you gotta dress up in paper clothes. It's really easy and they look so pretty.

We go to the café and have a big feed and even a chocolate milkshake. It's so nice that the boys want another but they can't. Lynnie and me laugh—serves them right for being greedy. We all start looking into the shops. The boys are allowed to look by themselves but us girls aren't. 'It's not fair! How come they can go by themselves?' Mummy tells us, 'Because they're boys'. I still think it's not fair. Sometimes, I wish I was a boy, too, then I could do lots more things as well.

Me, Mummy and Lynnie go into another shop and the shop assistant girl is nice. She asks me what I want: a doll or something else. I tell her, 'I don't know'. She points around at lots of different things. Just then, Mummy comes over and I look up on the wall and I see it. A little white dog. 'Mummy, look up there, the dog.'

Grabbing a big ladder, the girl arms herself with a stick and, climbing the ladder, gets it down. It's way up high. As I watch her, I hold my breath and then close my eyes real tight, whispering under my breath as I do, 'Please don't drop it. Please don't drop it.' I repeat it over and over again; my voice is in my throat but it doesn't want to make a noise.

She gets it down safely and passes it to me. I love it. My heart is bursting as I hold it close and feel it next to my skin. 'Oh, Mummy, it's beautiful.' The toy dog is white with a red tongue sticking out and it's got a big gold chain on it. Mummy asks me, 'How much is it?' I turn the price tag around, holding my breath, saying a little prayer at the same time, willing it to be under my four dollars and fifty cents.

Oh, no, it's five dollars fifty. I look at Mummy; I feel my heart breaking and my voice cracking as I try hard not to cry.

'It's okay. I'll pick something else.'

I hand it back to the girl and walk away. I move away from Mummy for a little while. I don't wanna let her see me with a broken heart. I don't want Lynnie to see me, neither. She would tease me for being a sook and then she would tell the boys and then I would really cop it.

When I'm ready, I sing out to Mummy, 'There's a doll over here, Mummy'. It's dressed in pink and real pretty. 'Santa can bring me this instead.' I point it out to her and go and find Lynnie. She's chosen a doll, too, but hers can walk and it comes up to my waist. She teases me because her doll will be bigger than mine.

We go home, all of us happy with our shopping and our presents that we picked out. I think of the dog and wonder what will happen to him. It's a wonderful afternoon, the sun is smiling and we are, too, 'cause we don't have to work. We don't even have to do any jobs tonight: no nothing. We can just rest.

Mummy's lying back reading the paper. She bought us all a game of snakes and ladders, and the boys are trying to cheat. It's been a good day. I'm tired, I wanna go to bed. It's three days to Christmas.

Then it's Christmas morning and Santa's been in the middle of the night. I don't know how he finds us and how he always brings the presents we pick out. I think, what a clever man he is, and I wonder how Mummy lets him know what we want. My mother, she's pretty smart, you know. I open all my presents: first, there's marbles and jacks, and some more paper dolls from Lynnie, and the boys bought me some play jewellery.

Lots and lots of presents just for me. I think I'm so lucky but I wonder where the little dog is now? We've all finished opening our presents and us kids show each other what we got. We're all excited and happy but I didn't get the doll from Santa. Lynnie got hers. Maybe he forgot—or maybe he thought I was bad so I couldn't have a special present like the other kids.

I hear Mummy talking to me.

'Kerry, there's one more present to open. Yes, it's yours!'

I think it must be the doll—Santa didn't forget—and that means I wasn't bad after all. Mummy passes my present to me. I feel it and can't help but shake it, wondering what it could be. I know it's not the doll—there's no box.

'Open it,' everyone says at the same time 'cause they all know. My fingers get a hold of the paper and it starts ripping.

'The dog! Mummy, I got the dog!'

Excited, I run to her and give her the best cuddle she's ever had in all her life. I show everyone my dog. The boys want to know if the tongue comes out. She tells them to behave and leave me alone. I pick up my dog and go outside. This is the best working Christmas I ever had.

27

Leeton Show and the Mormons

We go and live in a little flat in Leeton till the fruit-picking season is over. We're trying to earn as much money as we can to buy our own house somewhere. Big sister, Maureen, lives here in Leeton as well so that's good; she has a place down the road from us. She has three boys now and we love 'em lots. Me and Lynnie, we're allowed to help her with her babies which makes us feel so important and grown-up. We still try to avoid Sam, though.

Us kids love going down to her house. She still spoils us, plus she lives near the irrigation channels so we can swim there every day. One day, she got real sick and had to go to hospital. Sam takes Mummy to the hospital while us kids, we worry and wait at home. The doctors tell her a snake bit her—and she didn't even know it.

We've got my cousin, Billy, living with us now in Leeton. He's Uncle Paddy's boy by his first marriage to Aunty Frances, the one that first told us the news about our house getting burnt down. (Aunty Frances lives in Forbes and we still call in there on the way home from the paddocks all the time.)

We're going to church again, but this time, it's the Mormons. We go to them for about six months while we're in Leeton, this time doing the oranges. They're really nice. Mummy makes 'em a cup of Milo every time they come and visit. They're not allowed to drink tea or coffee so it's Milo instead. We've all gotta have it when they're here but Mummy loves her cup of tea. As soon as they're gone, we put the jug on. I don't think anyone could stop her drinking her cuppa tea. She wouldn't give it up, not for all the money in the world.

We go to church and put our money in the tin, but sometimes it's hard to do that; we need the money, too. We do it, anyway. Sometimes though, brother Paddy, he only pretends to put the money in there and keeps it instead. Then he buys us lollies to share. The Mormons baptise all us and cousin Billy, too, in the Murrumbidgee River which is just right for us 'cause we're river people.

The christening takes place five days after my tenth birthday: 29th October 1966. We all gotta dress in white, then they take us out in the water and dunk us under. I come up spluttering as they hold you down backwards so the water goes right up your nose. We have a big barbecue in the park when it's over. Lynnie loves Elder Hadley and I'm Elder Christianson's favourite. I'm in love with him, too. He's so tall—I only come up to his waist. I reckon there would have to be two and a bit of me to make one of him.

***

It's Show time here in Leeton but we can't afford to go. Mummy scrapes enough money together to buy some coloured crepe paper from the newsagent so she can make us some paper flowers which we can sell door-to-door. She makes some beautiful carnations—all different colours and so pretty.

We don't like knocking on people's doors and selling things much but we wanna go to the Show and Mummy says it's an honest living and there's nothing wrong with that. She tells us we have to sell in pairs. One of us has to stand out the front and play cockatoo and watch while the other knocks on the door. We're not allowed to let each other out of each other's sight.

Before we go into the front yard, though, we look to make sure there's no kids playing there. We would die of shame if any of our friends see us. We say a little prayer, begging that none of 'em live in any of these houses in these streets. If we come to a house and see any kids at the house or even a bike out the front or in the back yard, we walk straight past and don't go in.

I gotta knock while Lynnie plays cockatoo. I'm lucky this time. A lady answers. I ask her if she would like to buy some of my flowers. She asks me why I'm selling 'em. I tell her, 'So we can go to the Show'. She doesn't buy any flowers but gives me a dollar, anyway. It's funny, a lot of people give me money but don't buy the flowers. That's good 'cause we can sell the ones they don't take to someone else. We're so happy: we earn enough for all of us to go to the Show and we spend up real big and have lots of fun on the rides, too.

Selling the flowers is just like when we was back on the Island and we took all the empty drink bottles up to the shop. When we did that, we hoped our friends didn't see us cashing 'em in to get money, either. Meryl used to collect the most, so she sent us up to the shops with all these bottles in the pram and we had to buy milk and bread and slices of Devon sausage with the money the shopkeeper gave us; but it was good because she always made sure that there was enough for lollies for us.

Lynnie and me can't wait to get home to eat a piece of Devon, so we grab a slice each and roll it up and take a bite of yummy meat that makes our tummy happy. Afterwards, we try to wrap the paper around it so no one can tell we raided it.

Just like with the flowers, we always held our breath and prayed that nobody saw us doing it. One day, it was me and Lynnie's turn to cash the bottles in and we got caught by some of the town boys who made our life a misery, teasing us.

'Where's your baby?'

'She's asleep. Piss off !'

'Come on, let's see, where's your baby?'

'Lynnie, tell 'em to piss off.'

They stood in front of us; we stood in front of the pram, trying real hard to stop 'em seeing what was really in there. They tried to pull the blanket from over the bottles. We covered the bottles up so people would think we really did have a baby sleeping there. They pushed us outta the way and started to laugh at us.

'Haha, your baby's so pretty, isn't she?'

'What's her name?' they all laughed.

We swore at them all the time while they tormented us. They wouldn't go away and leave us alone; we threatened them with our big brothers. They finally went away but were laughing so loud we were sure we could still hear 'em down in the gutters on our way home. Shame job!

But we only stay living in Leeton till the fruit-picking is over, then we head home again.

Back in Condo, Daddy is back with us again. We stay in a house made into a flat just across the road from Meryl; she's gonna have another baby. School's okay and the kids are great. We all play together, us Blackfellas. One day, I was mucking around in class and the teacher came up behind me and hit me on the head with a book. I run home to Mummy and dob him in. She was up there at the school the next day, after that teacher. I heard her telling him straight, 'You don't hit my daughter. You send a note home to me if she mucks up but don't you ever hit her or I'll be back.' Mummy don't let no one hit us.

I'm in love with Elvis, still, and some of the other movie stars. I save all my pocket money to buy their magazines, then I rip 'em up and stick 'em up on the wall on my side of the room that me and Lynnie share. It's the first time in a long time that we've got a room to ourselves. Mummy and Daddy have a room and the boys, too. We think it's so great. We tell the boys they're not allowed in our room.

28

Morisset Mental Hospital

It's 1968 and I'm ten. We're gonna go and see our Dad again. We haven't seen him for a long while; Kevin and me are real excited.

Daddy's driving us up to see him so we're all really happy. This place isn't as scary as the last time; it's much friendlier and the people are nice, too.

We got to sit with him and talk to him and touch him! There was nothing stopping us. No walls or bars or wire mesh, just us and him sitting around this table. I was allowed to sit on his lap for the first time in my life. I wrapped my arms around his neck as he held me tight around the waist. I touched his hair. It's like mine—it's got curls, kinda like ringlets but he has more of them. I told him the story of Meryl and Maureen wrapping my hair with brown-paper strips and how, next morning, I had fuzzy hair and the kids called me a golliwog.

We had the best visit! We're real happy to see him. His eyes were still sad but they sparkled like mine when he got excited and laughed, and I could tell he's really happy. We talked and talked and held hands. We told him about school and all the rest of the family. He told us he'd be coming home one day. I don't think anyone wanted to leave that day. I reckon my Dad didn't want us to go at all. I could tell.

We argue about who looks like him the most and who's got the blackest hair as well, and we both win. My hair is black and a little bit curly like his; Kevin's is just black and straight. Mummy is happy, too. We all tell him how much we love him and miss him but then it's time to leave again. During my childhood, we only ever visited my father three times: the first time in Grafton Jail; this second visit in Morisset Mental Hospital; and a third time, later on, is at Long Bay Jail.

This trip has been so exciting and wonderful, and we seen all these new things and did things that we never do at home; we can't wait to tell the others. Another long drive in the car and then we're home again back in Condo, back where we belong. We run and kiss everyone, excited. Lots of family come over that night for a big feed and to find out how our trip went. Hooray!

In June 1968, he was moved again, to Long Bay Jail.

29

We got grandparents

Boy, I think when I hear the news, me and Kevin must be getting grown-up. Mummy asks me if I remember the port full of clothes that we had in Leeton before our hut burnt down when we were picking and Blue saved Maureen. I tell her, yes. She reminds me that they were from our grandparents. She tells us we're going to go and see them but we're not allowed to mention our father to them.

Mummy takes us over to where they live in Gulgong, the town on the ten-dollar note. She sleeps at their house for one night to settle us in, then she goes back home. Our grandparents don't say a word about our father, neither, but Nanna tells us about her daughter, Goma, who was our mother. She shows us pictures. She says not to mention Goma in front of Pop because he'd get upset. And she shows us pictures that Mummy has sent them of me and Kevin growing up. On the back of them, Mummy has written:

    Kerry (in front) and Kevin 2nd on right, playing marbles.
    'To our Nanna and Pop
    With love,
    Love Kevin and Kerry xxxx.'
    Kerry aged one.
    'To Nanna and Pop
    With love,
    Love Kerry xxx.'

Nobody tells us how my mother died. Mummy would've told my grandparents they weren't to say anything to us. Mummy, when she wants to, she can put the fear of God in anyone. I reckon even God himself if he was real.

I have lots of uncles here in Gulgong that are my mother's brothers. My favourite is Uncle Bob. He lets me drive his ute; I have to sit on his lap 'cause I'm too little. I'm nearly eleven and my feet don't touch the floor but I'm allowed to steer and change the gears.

In Gulgong, Kevin stays up at Uncle Lester's house most of the time. They have a son called Garry so the two boys play together. Anyway, they don't like me much and I don't like any of them much, neither, 'cause they pick on me. And my Aunty, she's always bossing me around, makes me wash up when the other kids are in the lounge room. Kevin and Garry never seem to wash up, only me. I ask her why and she tells me, 'Boys don't wash up, only girls'. I think, what a lotta bull; the boys gotta wash up at home. Mummy says, 'We all gotta learn how to cook and clean so we can take care of ourselves'.

I can't say this to her, though; I reckon she'd go crook on me. Then, I'd have to tell Mummy and then Mummy would go after her, and then there'd be trouble. And I don't want no trouble so nobody can tell Mummy I've been bad and I won't ever have to go away with the Welfare.

I stay with Nanna and Pop and Uncle Bob most of the time and they love me lots. Nanna says not to worry about the others, they don't like girls much. Nanna talks just a little about my mother when she was little and she shows me photos of the family.

I had a really good visit in Gulgong as I had a friend there, down the road from Nanna and Pop. We'd go swimming just about every day at the pool, and when we didn't do that, Nanna would take me to the shop and buy me and Kevin a little something like a lolly or a packet of special biscuits. Nanna would introduce us to the people she knew as, 'These are Goma's two'. She seemed real proud of us and our Mum.

Her and Pop even worried about what we was gonna eat for breakfast. They went and bought all these different packets of cereals so that we could try them all to find the one we liked best. Boy, we were spoilt!

We go to Sydney with Nanna and visit more of my mother's family there. My other family is big, too, but not as big as my family back home. I like my cousins in Sydney and have a great time but I wanna go home pretty soon; I miss Mummy so bad and I want my real family. We stay in touch with Nanna and Pop always but I don't remember another visit with them during the school holidays.

30

Koora: the little town on the railway track

Our big brothers have been trying to find another place for us to live. We need to buy a house so we can keep the Welfare from our door. One day, they tell Mummy they found us a place in a little town called Koorawatha. It's seventeen miles from Cowra and twenty-seven miles from Young. It's a good spot; we can pick the tomatoes one way and the cherries the other. And the prunes are close by and the tomatoes at Goolagong as well. We'll have the paddocks surrounding us; we'll always get work.

Mummy has worked and saved and now she goes to the bank to see if they will lend her the rest of the money to buy the house. They do and we all celebrate—our very own house again! I hear the others talking how the bank don't lend money to women by themselves but they lent money to her.

It's a big deal for us, especially since she's Aboriginal—she's well-respected and liked here in Condo. We're so lucky and so rich—a house all our own—and we've got the smartest and bestest Mother in the world. Daddy hasn't been with us for a long time now. We don't really worry; Mummy looks after us.

We're moving. We're gonna live in Koorawatha or Koora for short. We've got our house and it even has some acres to go with it! Mummy's so proud and so are we. Now, we don't have to travel so much to pick the fruit and the Welfare can't get us; we'll have our own house and he can't say nothing. And we don't have to live in flats no more or other people's houses; and we got the road to play on like we did on the Island as well so it's nearly as special as the Island was.

It's a bit rundown but it's gonna be a happy house; all of us are gonna be living there. Uncle Raymond comes to help us move. Him and Paddy do all the heavy lifting. Mummy helps as much as she can. We all do. Maureen's here, too, doing her bit. They put all the furniture inside the house and our clothes are packed away.

And we have a bathtub, too, with a little heater connected to it that you light to make a fire so you can have hot water. This one's not like the one Mummy has outside to do our washing in. That copper's like a giant pot and she lights the fire under it and boils our sheets and things so they're real white and clean. I love coming home and seeing our sheets blowing on our clothesline and I love my bed with nice clean sheets, too.

Uncle Raymond and my brother, Paddy, go up to the pub to have a drink after all the hard work of moving is done. It's Paddy's first time in a pub. Mummy let him go for one drink because he's with Uncle Raymond and he worked so hard moving us in. We don't have any drink at home. My older brothers are not allowed to bring drink into our house or even come home drunk. Mummy would've been real angry if they did.

It's only a little while later that we hear noises and lots of yelling coming from up the main street. She sends

Kevin up on his bike to see what's happening. She must have known something was wrong because she didn't wait for him to come back before starting to run in the direction of the noise. Maureen, who's got a big belly—she's six months' pregnant—started trying to run, too, following her. They knew straight away the men were in trouble. Mummy tells us kids to stay. Not to follow 'em. We stay and wait but they don't come back. Kevin jumps on his bike and follows them, not all the way, just to the park so he can see what's happening. He comes back.

'The pub—the whole pub—they're fighting with them, with Mummy and Maureen and Uncle Raymond and Paddy!!!'

The whole pub! They're fighting with our family! We run to help and we're halfway there but they're already on the way home. The men are smashed up a little bit but they say the other blokes in the pub look worse than they do.

They tell the story of how some blokes in the pub started making comments about Blacks, saying they don't want no Blacks living in their town and they don't want Blacks in their pub, either. They fought dirty, too. It wasn't man-to-man; they were like a pack of dogs on heat, Uncle Raymond said. He called them gutless bastards. They even wanted to fight Mummy and Maureen.

We wonder how a pub full of grown men wanna fight two women and even one that's gonna have a baby. We're angry, too, about them trying to bash Paddy and Uncle. We know they can take care of themselves but not when a whole town wants to fight 'em. Uncle Raymond laughs and says, 'Don't worry. I had two of 'em on me at one go and I couldn't move so I bit one man's ear so bad he'll probably need stitches.'

'Serves 'em right. They're a pack of dogs. Just like a pack of dogs on heat.'

I hope they hurt real bad. Us kids talk about it later and start laughing. Serves them right! We hope Uncle and Paddy flogged 'em really good. That'll teach 'em for fucking with the Blacks. Us kids all talk about 'em. We can fight with each other—that's all right—but no one else can. We hate this town already. We've only been here a little while, not even a day; just moved in and already they're causing us heartache.

***

But it's wonderful that we got our own house and it's easier for Mummy, too. If she's not working, she's always cooking us a special treat for when we come home from school. She cooks little cakes and pies with custard, too, and I get to have two lots 'cause the other kids don't get home from school till after me.

Us kids still help Mummy; we try to make things easier for her. Each Sunday, we have to pick a room out and clean it from top to bottom. The kitchen's the hardest to clean; we have to empty out the food cupboards and the knife-and-fork drawer, and put new newspaper on the shelves to make it all clean and tidy.

I'm twelve now so I go to the primary school here but Lynnie and Kevin gotta travel on the big bus to high school and back again, and that's a long way. They go twenty-nine miles each way to school and back. It's twenty-seven miles to Young but they gotta turn off the highway after eighteen miles and go one mile up to Bendick Murrell to pick up the kids there, then travel back down to the highway and keep going to Young. Every day, all that way, fifty-eight miles to school for the round trip.

31

Pay day and trains, and getting shot at

I think Mummy must be getting the pension; every fortnight now she gets a cheque. It's the first time in our lives that we haven't had to work our guts out and now we don't have to travel so much to do the fruit-picking. We can live. When we really need money bad, she sells one of her old coin collections. I know she hates doing that; she knows she's not gonna get the right amount of money for them off the man that buys them from her.

When pay day comes, Mummy and me catch the train to Cowra to get our groceries. It's a long way on the train but it's fun, plus it means I don't have to go to school. No way would Mummy let me stay home by myself in Koora after I get let out from school at three o'clock.

Koorawatha's full of people that hate Blacks. Even at school, some of the white kids don't talk to me. They write my name in the dirt and write things about me there. They make sure the teacher's not around, and when I walk out of class, there's a message calling me a Black gin and even some love letters, too. After a few swear words, the kids leave me alone 'cause I can beat most of them in a fight, I reckon, but I'm here by myself and I wish Kevin and Lynnie were here, too—I hate it on my own.

After school, I normally hide in the toilets till they're all gone and the coast is clear. Today, I start to go to the toilet to hide but then I see Mummy waiting outside in the rain. She's standing under a tree trying not to get too wet. She has a towel over her shoulders and one for me, too.

I'm torn; I don't want the other kids to see me but she's out there getting wet so I run to her and she covers me up with the towel. I give her a cuddle; I've got the best mother in the world. She has cooked a cake for me and she's gonna make me a Milo to warm me up while I dry off.

Heather Hampton becomes my best friend. She lives just up the road. Other than her family and a few others, most of the grown-ups here are real mean; they hate us Blacks. Even the policeman, Constable Saunders, he's as bad as the rest of the town. He ran our dogs over for nothing and they was only little ones. We cried forever. And they did terrible things to the rest of our animals. We had some pigs and somebody came and shot pellets into them, even into their teats. Mummy wouldn't let me look, but I was so sad. How can people do mean things like that?

One time, one of them even shot at Mummy. We've got a cow called Mini Moo, after Lynnie, and she had a calf. One day, Mummy went to feed 'em and the neighbour, Mrs D'Elboux, shot at her. The bullet went through her hair. Mummy went to see Constable Saunders, but he didn't wanna do nothing about it. He said, 'I'll talk to her'. He comes back and says to Mummy that Mrs D'Elboux thought that she was trespassing on their land. Mrs

D'Elboux knew it was our land—that's just an excuse. I hate this town.

Mummy wants her charged with attempted murder.

'She could've killed me!' she argues.

Constable Saunders still doesn't want to charge her. Mummy goes to the police station in Cowra and charges her herself. They go to court and Mrs D'Elboux gets community hours' weekend detention. I think they should've made her rot in jail for months but Mummy feels sorry for her; she's a little bit gwarnnee (mentally ill) and she has a new baby. I don't feel sorry for her. I hate her for trying to hurt my mother.

The people in this town persecute us: they stalk our house at night—we can hear them outside, laughing and talking, trying to scare us to leave town. When they do this, Mummy walks outside and sings out in a real loud voice, calling them gutless bastards and saying she'll blow their brains out if she catches them.

None of us kids are allowed to go anywhere after dark by ourselves. We can't even go out to the toilet at night;

even at dusk, we gotta go in twos and Mummy stands at the door and watches, but when it gets later, we use a bucket inside if we need it. We don't know what them whitefellas'll do to us if they catch us alone and especially at night, too.

Constable Saunders harasses us kids when we go to the shop or the disco they have at the town hall sometimes. He comes along and lets down the tyres on our bikes. We start arguing with him, telling him, 'You have no right. What about the other kids' bikes? They're standing right beside ours. Are you gonna let 'em down, too?'

He says our tyres are baldy and dangerous but it's not true: Kevin fixes our bikes all the time and he's good at it. After he leaves, we swear about him and call him 'Cuntstable Saunders'. We've gotta walk our bikes home. When we get home, we tell Mummy. She goes after him; she won't let people harass us, even if it's a policeman.

But she can't stop him from harassing us all the time, and eventually, she's had enough. She writes to his boss, she puts in a complaint. She tells his boss about Mrs D'Elboux, about Constable Saunders not charging her, how she had to go to Cowra and how he deliberately ran over our dogs, killing 'em. About the townspeople shooting our animals and stalking our house at night; and how Saunders picks on us kids whenever he sees us up the street without her.

He's in big trouble then and he don't like it. He comes to Mummy and asks her to withdraw the complaint but Mummy says, 'No. I hope you rot where you're going.'

We're happy to see the back of him and hope there's no Blackfellas in the town he's going to; they're gonna cop it real bad. The kids at school don't pick on me so much now. They must be getting used to having a Black gin going to their school. Me and Heather are still best friends.

32

Anzac Day and Martin Luther King

We're back in Condo temporarily; I think Meryl's having a baby again. I sing in the choir at school and I even sing with them on Anzac Day, down the main street. It's a public holiday but we all go to show our respect to the soldiers who fought in all the wars. When everyone is marching, I think Mummy wishes Daddy and Uncle Raymond were here to represent us as a family. Uncle Raymond still lives in Sydney with Aunty Una and their kids but I reckon Mummy wishes they were here so they could march, too. I know she's real proud of them both. Uncle Athol (Paddy and Lynnie's Dad) was in the war but he passed away down in Shepparton. Mummy was proud of him, too.

Uncle Raymond, especially. He was sneaked into the Army at sixteen when the laws of our country wouldn't let him because he was Aboriginal. All my Uncles weren't allowed to enlist because they were Aboriginal but ours did. He wasn't supposed to be in the war but he stole Mummy's birth certificate and pretended he was older than he was. Uncle Raymond was fairer-skinned so he was able to sneak in. A lot of other Aboriginal men went, even with the law banning Blacks from serving in the army. They went because it was our country, too.

    One day, after we've been living in Koora for about six months, I get invited to the birthday of Colleen from school. Mummy takes me to town on the train to buy a new dress and a present. When the day comes, she gets Lynnie to walk me halfway and I'm allowed to walk the rest of the way to Colleen's house by myself, and I'm feeling so good. This is the first time I've ever been to a birthday party that doesn't belong to one of my family. I walk, so happy, smiling like the world was just meant for me. I round the corner near her house and her father's standing on their front verandah. He yells at me, 'Get home, you Black slut! We don't want your kind here.'

I run away, crying. I head to the railway silos and I hide. I rip the present apart and chuck it in the grass. Nobody's gonna have it now. I sit and wait, crying. I can't go home and tell Mummy; she would go after him. Then, there'd be trouble again and she might really get hurt this time.

I watch the sun slowly going over the sky till I think it's time to go home. I walk in the house smiling. Mummy asks me, 'Did you have a good time? Did she like her present?' I lie through my teeth and tell her, 'Yes, it was great and everyone was real nice'.

***

It's 1968. In other places, the hippies and the peace movement are in full swing but, in Koora, our news is that Mummy's gonna get her licence and then get a little car. We won't have to go on the train no more and it will save us camping all the time while we're doing the prunes and tomatoes; we can drive there each day. The car is a little red Hillman Hunter. My nieces and nephews sing songs about her and the car.

'Here comes Ma in her little red wagon, jumping up and down, and the rear end dragging.'

It's a funny little song and Mummy loves it. Now, we can go to Condo to see all the family. It takes us five hours because Mummy refuses to drive over forty miles per hour and, along the way, we have pit stops for cuppas from the thermos. We can go to bingo, too. Mummy loves bingo and usually she wins, not a lot, but just what she needs. She always says, 'I need this much to buy Kevin a pair of shoes and I need this much for petrol to get us home and this much for tucker'. And she wins it, sometimes not enough for everything, but most times she does, anyway. I know she says a little prayer to God to help her now and again.

One day in April, us kids are at home watching TV and Mummy comes in the room and turns it off. We're upset; we wanted to watch but she tells us that Dr Martin Luther King got shot down today and we had to show some respect for this man which means no TV.

We all know who he was. He was a special Black man in America who fought for human rights for Black people. We have heard him on TV and my favourite is when he says, 'I have a dream'. We want a dream here, too, for Aboriginal people. It hasn't changed much in this place, I reckon, for us or for the Blackfellas over in America, either, since President Kennedy got shot.

We don't mind showing this man respect. He deserves it and, anyway, when any of our family members pass away, Mummy does the same thing. The TV's not allowed to go on and it stays off until she decides we're allowed to have it on again. We go into our rooms, knowing we have to be quiet. Being quiet when people are talking is respectful and being quiet when someone has died is respectful, too.

My big sister [actually Kerry's cousin but they all live together with Kerry's Aunt whom Kerry calls 'Mummy'], Meryl, is having troubles with her baby so I have to go and help her in her house in Condo. Mummy drives over and stays for a night, and then heads back to Koora. I go back to Condo school and help Meryl when I come home in the afternoons. It's just before Easter and I'm sleeping in the lounge room. My big brother [actually Kerry's cousin], Darryl, is staying there, too. Something about Darryl makes me feel like spiders are crawling over my skin. I try to avoid him the best I can.

***

When Meryl is a little better with the baby, Mummy comes to take me home to Koora. I'm glad. If Mummy thinks I'm a bad girl, the Welfare might come and take me away. I sit terrified in the back of the car, not talking or laughing or even singing any songs.

Mummy knows something is wrong.

She tells the other kids to go and put the jug on. I tell her I'm bleeding inside. She sings out to Lynnie to come and get me to take me in the house. She tells me, 'Lynnie'll show me what to do'. I have my periods; there's nothing to worry about, it's normal. I breathe a sigh of relief. I'm not gonna be sent away. The Welfare won't come; it's only my periods.

***

Meryl gets sick with the baby again so I go back to help her. The Condo school carnival is on and I love sports; all us kids are good at what we do. I love the high jump and I come second place in the Senior High Jump. And it's great that I'm a senior at my school. I run home to Mummy to show her my certificate. I tell her how much I got beat, 'Only by one inch, that's all,' and how it wasn't just the Condo kids I was jumping against but all the other kids from the schools from all over the bush.

The certificate—it's got my name on it but they spelt Kerry wrong. I take a pen and change the '-ie' to a '-y'. Mr Readon's one of my favourite teachers and I can't believe he spelt my name wrong. He dates it, 9th August 1968.

In October, we're all camped at Meryl's and my thirteenth birthday is tomorrow. I'm sleeping in the lounge room again. I'm so happy. When I wake up, I've got a piece of string tied to my finger and I gotta follow it to find my present. The string goes into the kitchen, it goes around the bread canister, around the toaster, down and out of a cupboard, out into the laundry and it's still not ending.

The string, it's going everywhere. I'm so excited! I follow it out the back door and under the lemon tree and orange trees up along the back fence into the flowers. Finally, I come to the end, lying there with the Lily of the Valley. I've found a little box on the end of the string. I gotta watch, my very own watch! Mummy tells me that now that I'm getting ready for high school next year, I need my own watch to tell the time.

I thank her so much for my watch and I tell her how much I loved playing the game of following the string and finding it in amongst the flowers. She got the kids to put the string everywhere but told them to leave the present in the flowers. I tell her I like the Lily of the Valley and she says she does, too, and that 'They were your mother's favourite flowers'.

My mother's favourite flowers—wow, this is cool. I know something else about my mother. We head back to Koora after a couple of days and back to Koora primary school. I can't wait to be in high school. What's more important, I'm gonna be the youngest in my family ever to go to high school. My cousin, Rachel, is gonna come and live with us. She's younger than me so I won't be the baby anymore; but that's all right—we love her heaps. She has to sleep with me in the room with Lynnie.

Darryl's also moving in to live with us. I think Mummy thinks we gotta have a man here to help protect us from the town; they're still giving us hell. I wish he wasn't, though. He's working in Cowra at Edgell's Cannery, though, so that's good. We don't see him much and, when we do, we try to stay away from him.

33

Mother's Day and White Trash

It's Mother's Day and we've got no money to buy Mummy a present. There's no work around, either, but Mummy has an account at the Koora General Store; and we're allowed to book up a present each for her on her bill. There's nothing real pretty in that shop but I find a big silver alarm clock that has a bell on top and rings real loud. I think it's a great present for Mummy so I buy her that, take it home and wrap it up.

I give it to her and she loves it, so I'm happy. But it's real funny, I don't think us kids ever paid our bill at the store—only Mummy.

Mummy sends me to Cowra High School but I don't like it. I wanna go to school with Kevin and Lynnie and Heather; I wanna go to Young. I tell her and she lets me go there instead. We keep heading back to Condo regularly for family occasions. When the school holidays come, we still do the fruits.

Meryl's having her fourth baby and we're all hoping for a boy. She has three girls and they're all beautiful but a little boy would be special. Meryl hasn't got a washing machine and has been bending over the bathtub washing the clothes. She nearly loses the baby so I go back to help her. This time, Darryl's not around and so I feel safe. Meryl does have a little boy.

Mummy bought me my very own camera for my fourteenth birthday and I'm so happy. I love photos as much as she does and I wanna takes lots of the family. I can only take pictures in black and white since coloured photos are too dear; and I only get a little bit of pocket money unless we're picking. I guess my family's just gonna have a lotta black and white photos.

I get to be like Mummy; I don't like leaving my photos at home when we travel. I put them with Mummy's in the pretty Arnott's biscuit and lolly tins in the back of the car, just to make sure.

That way, if there's a fire again, they won't get burnt.

***

Big brother, Johnny, and his wife, Beryl, and their kids are living with us in Koora now. Cousin Rachel's gone home to Uncle Paddy and Aunty Carol, and Darryl has moved into Cowra for work. I'm not sorry to see him go.

Aunty Doris, Mummy's eldest sister, and her kids, have moved to Koora, too. Aunty Doris is just like Mummy; she works real hard so she can keep her kids happy. She's lovely and soft and kind. Mummy always says she's the soft one in the family. Loretta goes to school with me. She's the same age and she's in my class. Sharon's my other cousin; she's the same age as Lynnie. Us girls all hang around together; there's Lynnie and Sharon, me and Loretta and my best friend, Heather. We walk around like this little gang of girls.

We don't do bad things, just fun things like teasing the boys. When we're all together, we call ourselves 'We, Us & Co.' We wear a yellow T-shirt with all our names on the back and 'We, Us & Co.' written on there, too, and a pair of cut-off jeans. We all think we're real cool, and boy, do we strut!

Some of the grown-ups in town, they're still bastards—the ones who hate us for being Black. Most of the white kids are good now but there's still a couple who hate us, just like their parents do. One day, me and Heather are walking up the main street to the shops. One of the boys calls me a 'Black slut' as I walk past. I go to go after him but he runs. I yell after him, 'I'm gonna flog you when I get ya!' Heather says not to worry—we can get him on the bus tomorrow.

The next day, I wait till the afternoon. Just as we're pulling into Koora, I walk up to him. I've cooled down by now but I tell him, 'If you ever call me that again, I'll flog ya'. Me and Heather walk off the bus, laughing. I would've got in trouble if I started on him in the bus. Mr Brown would've barred me from the bus for a week and then I would've been in trouble with Mummy, too.

The next day, all is good in the world and I ignore him; the bus to and from school is good. Pulling into the bus stop at Koora, I see his mother, Mrs Worth—she's waiting for me to get off the bus. She screams at me, 'How dare you call him White Trash'.

I tell her, 'He called me a Black slut. I can call him what I like if he wants to call me names.'

She hits me right across the face and starts pulling my hair.

I hit her back.

Cousin Loretta is trying to stop the fight and attempts to pull me off this big fat woman. Mrs Worth has her hands full of my hair and, every time she pulls, more hair comes outta my head. She's got handfuls but I keep punching her in the face anywhere that I can connect. My hate and anger, all wrapped up inside me, comes out as I flog her for every racist comment and act this town has done to me and my family. I belt her and belt her. She'll never hit me again.

I go home to Mummy; I'm not too badly hurt, except for scratches on my face and less hair up top. When Mummy goes after her, she tells Mummy she's charging me with assault. She's got two black eyes and I'm glad. Mummy goes to the police and charges her, instead, with hitting me—a minor—a grown woman, twice my size and married with kids. The law wouldn't be happy with her.

Us kids laugh. A big grown fat woman like that charging me with assault. What a joke. The judge only has to take one look at the size of me compared to her and know that she did wrong hitting me in the first place.

Mrs Worth comes to Mummy and says, 'What do you want, to drop the charges?' I'm sure Mummy tells her to leave town and make sure her kids don't come near us or she'll charge her. They did and they don't! 'Serves them right,' we laugh. We're showing this town not to fuck with the Blacks. We won't run away from them. We'll stand up and fight each step of the way.

The racism in town quietens down. They stop picking on a single Aboriginal woman and her four kids, or at least, they're not so blatant now. We still hate the mad D'Elboux woman, though. We'll never forgive her for shooting at Mummy. We let her family know we don't like her and they let us know they don't like us, neither. Mummy tells us to stay away from them and we do, but if we see them, we give them dirty looks and make a smart comment.

34

A letter from the Queen

One day, it's my turn to pick the mail up from the post office and there's a letter from the Queen. Mummy, she's forever getting these special letters, official government letters with the Queen's emblem stamped in the corner. It's a big blue envelope telling the world it's real important; it says, 'On Her Majesty's Service'. It don't need a stamp like other letters so that makes it different.

As I pass it to her, I ask, 'What are these letters from the Queen for, Mummy?'—I'd seen so many before. She said, 'I wrote to the Queen and asked her to let your father out of jail. I write every year.' I ask her what she said to the Queen; I think it's so wonderful that she wrote to a real important person. I ain't never heard of anyone writing to the Queen before.

Mummy tells me that she asked the Queen to take into account how long my father's been in jail and what kinda life he had, and what was happening here in Australia for Aboriginal people back in those days. I try to imagine what she would've written and what her handwriting on the paper would have looked like. She had scrawly writing and, sometimes, it's even hard for me to read and I'm the best at reading. Maybe, my child's reasoning went, the letter might have said:

    To Her Majesty, the Queen,
    Dear Madam,
    I am writing to you in relation to my brother, Kevin; he is in jail. I am rearing up his two children, Kevin and Kerry. They need to have their father home with them and they need to know their Dad, every child needs their father.
    I know what my brother did was wrong but he was orphaned at the age of seven when we lost our parents. Since then, life has been hard for him. He's an Aboriginal man and, in those days, in this

country, life was hard for Aboriginal people.

I ask you to release my brother; he has been in jail now for a long time as punishment. He does not deserve to be in there anymore. He needs to be home with his children so that they can know their father.

Yours Sincerely.

Joyce Hutchings

(Signed and dated)

Mummy was such a proud woman, never asking for anything of anybody, but here she is begging the Queen to release her baby brother. In my mind, I can't write in the letter about what he's done 'cause I still don't know. All I know is that it was something bad and he's in a place for bad people, just like the Welfare puts bad kids in Homes and takes them away from their parents. My father did something bad and they took him away from us kids and his family. You don't have to understand the reasons for authorities to do what they do to be afraid of them.

Mummy goes to her room and stays there for a long time. She comes out, eventually, but doesn't say a word. I'm too scared to ask. She's not happy but she tells me, 'One day, your father's gonna come home; he's gonna come home to you and Kevin'.

I get little snippets of information now about my Dad. Not a lot, just a little bit now and again. Sharon, my cousin, sings, 'The Green, Green Grass of Home' and tells me that the song's for me. 'It's for your father, Uncle Kevin.' But I know it's about my mother, too. I can feel it in my heart. Is she supposed to be Mary, hair of gold and lips like cherries? I don't know. What's the tall oak tree mean? Are they gonna hang him under some tree? I just get so confused and I wanna scream out loud, *Somebody, tell me! I gotta know!* The thought doesn't enter my head that I have a right to know.

Sharon's got a beautiful voice; it's like the words drift in the wind real soulful and sadness is all over her face as she begins to sing. I listen to the words and feel sad deep down inside as well. Still nobody tells me why he's in jail. I am thirteen years old.

***

One day, Mummy says there's a show gonna be on TV about our father. Aunty June, Mummy's younger sister, along with a group of white women, are trying to get him out of jail. Lynnie and Paddy aren't allowed to watch the TV show; only me, Kevin and Mummy. She closes the lounge-room door so the others can't hear and can't see.

We're watching Aunty June talking on the riverbank. She tells how my father and her and Mummy and all their other brothers and sisters became orphaned—my Dad was only seven. They were living at Three Ways in Leeton when their own parents died.

Mummy's crying. Her mother had made her promise that if anything happened to her, she was to take care of the family. She's sobbing and I don't know what to do as I sit and feel tears roll down my face.

Our white Pop is on the show, too. He's telling them that my father deserves to rot in jail. I see his face, his torment there for all to see, his anger built up for years; his hate for him blazes from the television.

They zoom the camera into a dark night, a lonely road. My father begins to talk about my mother and why he killed her. Before he says a word, through her tears, Mummy keeps saying over and over again, 'Don't you believe what they're saying! It's lies—your mother was a good girl'.

I'm shattered by what my father says next. My father, on television, tells the entire world I am not his child; that my mother was running around on him. I know it's wrong because I looked so much like him the times we visited him in jail. I feel Mummy's heart breaking as we hear the shotgun blasts that take my mother's life away, through the volume of the television.

My father says he was a Black man in a white man's court and he had killed a white girl—the worst thing he could do. He says that the courts never took into account the circumstances. I hear none of this, just the words over and over again, *she's not mine.* But I look like him! He musta got it wrong; he's my father.

I can't help crying but I'm crying for my family. For Mummy. Not for my mother or my father but for Mummy. Her whole life has been for her family, for her kids, his kids. She would've believed that she had let her parents down and her brothers and sisters, too. Now Kevin Gilbert, my father, has told on the TV show about the hidden secret of his own parents' deaths back at Three Ways.

It was another taboo subject for the family that nobody talked about it. Our grandfather, a white man, shot our Aboriginal grandmother and then turned the gun on himself—a murder-suicide. My father, Aunty Flora and Aunty June were there when it happened. Aunty June ran to get Mummy and Aunty Doris. Now, it's out there for the world to see and know—Mummy is devastated.

I don't even cry for me and Kevin. We've got our life. I haven't missed out on much. I've got Mummy and my family. Mummy, her tears don't stop, not for one moment. She has to relive the memories of all these deaths again, the hurt and the pain. I cry for us all.

Mummy says that we're not to talk to anyone about the TV show. She tells us, again, that our mother was a good girl and that my father was drunk and angry. She says, if people ask, we are to say nothing, just tell them they have to ask her—Mummy. I know nobody would be game to do that.

The people in Koora do mention the show to us now. They all think Aunty June is Mummy but I tell them, no, that wasn't her at all.

And now my brother, Kevin, hates me. He believes our father's lies; that I'm not his child. He blames me for our mother's death.

I can't understand how my father could say I wasn't his when I look just like him. Did he hate me when I was a baby because my hair was blonde and not black like his? I look like my brother, too—you can tell we're brother and sister—so how can he say that? I scream loud inside at both of them, 'I've got black hair now!'

Big brother, Paddy, knew what was going on. He was always trying to protect me from the other two; if he caught them giving me heaps, he would give them heaps. They didn't pick on me when he was around. My big brother was my protector all my life. It was strange how Lynnie and Paddy are real brothers and sisters, and Kevin and me are real brothers and sisters but it was always the other way around; Lynnie and Kevin, Paddy and me.

I search now for other information about the death of my mother. Mummy's out fruit-picking, doing the tomatoes at Goolagong. I know I can't ask her for information; I don't want to make her cry again. Sister Maureen's the best—she'll tell us things if we ask but we gotta ask first. I wait for her to come and visit. She still spoils us a real lot; we love Sunny Boy ice blocks so she always buys them for us. I ask her about my mother. She was only ten when it happened, she says. Meryl knows better than her but Maureen tells me what she knows.

She tells me how the Old Man, Kevin, was a womaniser; he was seeing another woman while he was married to my mother and that's what started the fight. He was drinking with Daddy and some others, playing cards, and he started fighting with her. So, when the card game ended and it was time to go home, they left in the panel van with me and Kevin. Afterwards, he drove us all back to Mummy.

35

Hearing the stories of my mother

People talk a little bit more now about my real mother and father; just not when Mummy's around. Maureen's good about talking to us kids. She lives in Wagga Wagga with her boys and her husband, Sam, is in the army.

Maureen tells me how, after my mother was killed, we was all living out at Trundal and Daddy was working on the railway. Kevin had to sleep with Maureen because we didn't have enough beds. Maureen says that, one night, she woke up to our dead mother's spirit standing over the bed crying.

Maureen called out to Mummy and she rushed in and found that Kevin was real sick—he was gonna die. Mummy and Daddy raced down to the railway track and got him on the goods train to Condo, to the hospital, just in time. The train comes at midnight every night and it's the only one. He had pneumonia and a really high temperature. The doctor told Mummy that, if they hadn't caught that train, he would've died. So our dead mother's spirit saved my brother's life.

I listened, wrapped up in this story, soaking in each word, picturing this woman who gave birth to me. I know her a little bit in my mind but not a lot in my heart. I smile, proud that she saved my brother, happy he's alive because of her. I picture her as Maureen is talking. A beautiful woman in a pretty white dress with long hair and a hanky held to her face as tears roll down her cheeks; standing over my sick brother, knowing that there is nothing that she can do to save her firstborn.

Tears well up in my eyes and I gotta take a deep breath. Maureen says that, after it happened, she mainly took care of Kevin and Meryl looked after me; they had to help Mummy, as well. Kevin would cry, asking for his mother and he would talk about all the blood that was around. He was older than me so he remembered things.

She tells me how, when they were burying my mother, they were gonna bury her as a pauper—that means that the government would pay for her funeral—and that they laid a red rag on her coffin to say my mother died a poor woman with nothing. But Mummy and Daddy came to the funeral and seen the red rag and told them to take it off, that they would pay for her burial. Maureen tells me, 'They paid two quid a month outta Daddy's pay—he was a fettler on the railway—until it was paid off '. She don't know if my Nanna and Pop, my mother's parents, or her brothers came to the funeral. She can't remember.

As we're getting older, we hear rumblings from the big ones. We have always been dimly aware of murmurings: the older ones resenting us younger ones; how, if Mummy never took us on, things would have been easier for everyone. How the older ones blame us because they had to go without now and again so that we littlies always had food and clothes on our backs.

It's out in the open now. Animosity, hate, the whole lot. Hate from inside our family and hate from my father's. His documentary gave people permission to make our life a misery; our lives changed forever after that. Again, I hear the whispers about murder and Aboriginals. Some of the people in Koora are still trying to find out for sure if that was Mummy's brother on the TV. Mrs Friend asked me the other day, again, if that was Mummy sitting on the riverbank. I tell her, 'No'. She said, 'It sure looked like her'.

***

I know now why Mummy wouldn't let anybody tell us the truth before. She knew what we was gonna cop, not only from strangers but from the family as well. Life's a misery sometimes if you don't know if you belong or not. I know how much I love my family and I know in their hearts they love me, too, but sometimes it's real hard if they get mean and say things that hurt.

Sister, Meryl, tells me what she knows about my mother as well. She talks about how my Mum was real kind.

One time, Aunty June was having to look after Meryl as well as her own daughter, Cheryl. Aunty June would lock the two of them in the flat in Sydney and go to work and leave them there by themselves. One day, my mother came home and found them there alone so then she changed her work hours so she could take care of them. Everybody says the same thing; how kind and wonderful she was. Even big brother, Johnny, says so.

Sometimes now, I wonder what it would've been like if my real mother hadn't died, if my Dad hadn't killed her but my thoughts are fleeting. I don't really mind being Mummy's. And those times of wondering only really happen when someone gives me a hard time about not being Mummy's.

***

It's 1970 and I'm close to fourteen. After we pick the cherries in Orange, we call in and see our grandparents but we don't stay there by ourselves no more. They want to stay in touch, though. They still don't talk about my mother but, one day, Nanna gave me my mother's doll. It's real old and made of porcelain and got these real old clothes on. I treasure it. Years later, it got broken and I lost it amongst the travels. A big regret.

36

Nearly fifteen

Every year, we go and visit family that live on the Erambie Mission. Mummy has to get permission from the Mission Manager to enter the Mission. He always lets her, though. It's wonderful visiting. Mummy and Aunty Gwenie sit and have their cups of tea and I sit and listen to them talk or I go and play with the other kids. We got a big family and they live everywhere; not just in Condo and Koora but all over—I'm real proud.

But Mummy's worried about dying and I don't know why. When we're driving home, she tells me, 'If anything happens to me, you've gotta push me outta the way and stop the car as best you can and get out'. I'm not to worry about her but I gotta make sure I'm safe. I don't know why she's telling me this but I say, 'Yes, Mummy'. Now, I watch her like a hawk when she's behind the wheel, making sure she's all right, worrying if anything's gonna happen to her.

I'm too scared to ask the others why she'd be worried. It's like the fear with the Welfare: if I ask, it might come true. I know she had cancer years ago. That's why she was in hospital those times, why the other kids had to go to the Homes till she got better and why she was sick when we was living in the tents. Biting my lip, I worry.

There's a talent quest on at the Koora hall, put on for us young ones around town. Me, Lynnie and Kevin go. We have fun. Me and Loretta and Heather sing 'Daddy Cool' and come second. Some boys have taken Lynnie's shoes and we're trying to get them back; we'd get in trouble if she came home without them. Mummy has heard the ruckus from the hall; she thinks they were my shoes because she heard me singing out about them. I try to tell her they weren't, but Lynnie and Kevin say I'm lying. Mummy believes them and I get a hiding with the jug cord; my first-ever hiding, for doing nothing wrong.

I hate them for getting me in trouble for nothing. I can't believe that Mummy didn't believe me. Meryl comes over and asks me why I'm mucking up so bad. I don't try to explain 'cause I know she wouldn't believe me, either.

One day, after picking tomatoes out at Goolagong, I go down to the old, rundown wooden toilet away from the house. I sit and pretend to be going to the toilet while, all the time, I'm having a smoke. Because there's holes and cracks in the old wood, I wave my hands around trying to blow the smoke away so that, if Mummy's outside, she can't see none coming from inside the toilet.

I finish my smoke and walk back to the house. As I walk in, Mummy says, 'Come here to me, Miss'. I know instantly I'm in trouble.

'What have you got there?'

'Nothing, where?'

'In your pocket.'

'Nothing's in my pocket.' I look down and find my cigarette packet sticking halfway out of my jean pocket. I feel myself dying inside; now I know

I am in deep trouble. I hold my breath, not knowing what to say, what to do.

'Give them to me,' Mummy says. I pull them out and pass them to her. I know I'm gonna cop it. I try to reach out as far as I can so she can take them but it doesn't matter—she clips me under the ear. I hurt, not so much from the physical slap, but because Mummy had caught me doing something wrong. My ear is still ringing when I go into my bedroom crying, shattered. I have been Mummy's little Miss Goody-Two-Shoes all my life and now things have changed. I lie on my belly, shell-shocked that Mummy found those cigarettes.

After a while, I get up. My mood has changed. I'm pissed off now 'cause I lost my smokes. How am I gonna get another packet? I spent all my tomato money on them; I won't get no more till next weekend when we go to the paddocks again.

I look down at my hands. They're a mess; look at my nails—too many tell-tale signs of being a fruit picker. I feel myself getting wild with Mummy. If she wasn't in the kitchen when I walked through, I could've got the smokes to my bedroom and hid them. I start doing my nails. I feel better. I start singing one of them country and western songs. I do one hand and the next. I hear Mummy sing out to me.

I go out of the room happy. I'm over it now, having the shits with Mummy. I'm gonna make her a cup of tea. I grab the teapot and put the tea leaves in, waiting for the jug to boil.

Lynnie comes in.

'What're you doing?'

'Making Mummy a cup of tea.'

'Yeah, that's right! Mummy's baby, hey.'

'Fuck off, okay.'

I stand in front of the jug, willing it to hurry up and boil faster before anyone else comes in to give me shit. I was making the tea 'cause I love her, not to get in her good books. It takes more than that, anyway. My mind's thinking now: will Mummy think I'm making her a cup of tea just to suck up? I add the sugar and the old Sunshine milk. God, I hate that stuff in tea. I take it out to her.

'Mummy, I made you a cup of tea.'

'Thanks, daught.' All is right with the world.

Faintly, I hear Kevin sing out to me, 'Kerry, Heather's here'. I run out the door. She's got her denim gear on, too—I love it when we hang around together and dress the same. I get her and me a can of Coke each out of the fridge and we go outside to sit under our favourite tree. Heather tells me they went to town and did shopping, and she ran into the Buckleys—some of the other kids we hang around with—while she was there.

37

A fight and a visitor

We keep picking the fruits during the holidays. Old Great Uncle Paddy comes picking with us this year; it's wonderful. Mummy loves her family so much. I take a picture of them with their fruit-picking bucket hanging over their shoulders beside the tractor with the crate full of oranges. When we do the oranges, we have to stay over at Leeton and camp, usually in the boss's quarters. One time, we had a house, a proper house to stay in, and we couldn't believe it. Not a humpy, not a hut or an old train. A house! Boy, how lucky were we?

And then, on weekends we used to sell the oranges door-to-door. It was just like when we had to sell the flowers. We hated it 'cause now we were bigger, too, and the kids we went to school with treated us real bad and said rotten things. We tell Mummy and she says to tell them, 'It's an honest living'.

We still go to pick at Matt's in Orange and Gegg's in Young each year. It's easy at Gegg's 'cause it's out on the highway at Young and we only have a one-minute bus ride to school. Not like when we are at Koora and then we gotta go for miles. We sell the cherries, too, door-to-door. Gegg and Matt don't charge us for them. They let us pick the ones leftover on the trees but, boy, that's hard work 'cause you may only get a handful left on one tree and it could take you twenty trees to fill your bucket.

Johnny and Beryl and all the kids are living with us; we all pack into the little house at Koora. We're not so happy now. The house is too crowded and Johnny's real bossy, like Darryl.

***

It's 1971 and my Dad is being released from jail! He's coming home after spending fourteen and a half years away from us. Days go by and we wait and wait. Mummy tells us, 'Don't worry, he'll be here soon'. Still, we wait and wait. Then, one day, Mummy's reading the paper; she finds a picture of him.

She sings out to me and Kevin. We've gotta come inside, she has something to show us.

She tells us we're not to get upset but our Dad's in the paper. She shows us his picture. He's gotta woman with him. We can't believe it. He wouldn't do that to us; he said he was coming home and so did Mummy. He's married. He won't be coming home now. We've been waiting for him all our lives, all for nothing.

I'm devastated. He could've written. We had no telephone—there's only the one up the main street at the post office that we can use—but he could've written and told us, anyway. I think Kevin is angrier than me, though. I hurt to see my brother hurting so bad. I ask Mummy about it. She says, 'Boys need their father more than girls do'.

It's the weekend. We're not working but we're not allowed to leave the house for some reason. Mummy tells us we're having a special visitor today. She's excited, she's tidying up again.

He's here! It doesn't matter that he's married, he's here, he really did come home! We meet him, him and

Cora, his new wife, who is Dutch. He met her while he was in jail. She writes for the *New Dawn,* the Aboriginal magazine.

She wants to take pictures of us kids being reunited with our father. Mummy's angry. She tells them, NO! She says, 'We've been persecuted enough. They're not going to put our picture in no magazine for all of Australia to know what we look like and for nobody to hurt us.'

My father and Cora don't seem very happy about this and it feels a bit awkward, but they all have cups of tea and a talk. It's time for him to go and see Aunty Doris and her family. He'll be coming back again in a little while.

He visits the rest of the family and then he comes back to the house. This time everyone is so happy—it's like a new visit. Mummy, I haven't seen her smiling so much, fussing over him. It's like the whole world started smiling; the little brother came home to his big sister's and our Dad came home to us.

After about an hour, it's time for them to go. Mummy cries as she watches him walk away. We can't believe it. He was here a minute ago and now he's gone. We can't understand why he had to go so quick but he's on the way to Condo to see all the family there. We are all hurting deep down inside.

Mummy's sad and she tells us kids that he deserves a new start in life and, not to worry, he'll be able to come and see us all the time now. But Kevin's angrier than he's ever been in his life. He can't wait to get outta this place. I think he's angry about our Dad going and he reckons the photos wouldn't have mattered much. I think, though, he's just hurting all the way through because our Dad didn't come home to stay, like he was meant to.

Looking back, I think our Dad was supposed to be the pot of gold at the end of the rainbow for all of us: Mummy, 'cause her little brother finally came home to be a little brother again; and me and Kevin, well because he was supposed to be a father to us that he never was. But the pot of gold at the end of the rainbow after fourteen and a half years, it was a lie. It was more like a storm brewing before he came home and it sure wasn't gonna be no rainbow now and, since his death, it has been just that.

I wish I had been the oldest kid outta me and Kevin. I think I could've coped better with it than him. The whole bit, our mother being dead, our father in jail, then him supposed to be coming home and then he didn't. Kevin's so unhappy. We all are.

Kevin wants to go and live with sister, Maureen, but Mummy won't let him. She tells him he has to get his Fourth Form Certificate, then he can go. He's a real battler, my brother. He struggles at school but stays, determined to do it. He does, and we're all so proud when he gets his certificate in the mail; Mummy is bursting with pride. He leaves us then and goes to live in Wagga with Maureen.

38

The cherry pickers and the Tent Embassy

Mummy has bought another house for us in Koora. It's on the other side of the railway track, closer to Aunty Doris. Her and Mummy still work hard out in the paddocks. Wow, this house is flash; well, not that flash but pretty flash, and for the first time in my life, I have my own bedroom. I put my mother's porcelain doll on my bed each day after I've made it. I take out a couple of smokes and hide the packet in my undies' drawer and head to school.

I'm the last one at home and the last one at school, and I'm pretty spoilt. I love Coke and, every day, Mummy gives me two bob (20 cents) so that I can get a can. Boy, I think I'm in heaven! Beryl and Johnny still live with us—they have the sleep-out on the side of the house. One day, I come home from school and my mother's doll is ruined. Her head is all smashed in. I'm cranky and I go out demanding to know what happened. Me and Beryl have an argument. She says the kids went in there and did it, but I know she goes in there looking for my smokes. We swear at each other and call each other names.

Mummy comes home and Beryl dobs me in for swearing at her. I tell Mummy about my doll, so she has a go at Beryl and tells her they aren't allowed in my room and that the doll was special. I just want a normal life. I wanna go to school with nobody saying things about my family; I wanna be a teenager like every other teenager I know.

***

Our father's in our life now although we don't see him much. We're real proud of him, though, and I know Mummy is especially. When I was fifteen, he was living in Sydney and Lynnie was living there, too. She was gonna star in my father's play, *The Cherry Pickers.* I went to Sydney for a visit. He takes us to a Chinese restaurant in a place called Chinatown and it was up some stairs and really flash with red and gold splashed everywhere. My father orders this fancy tucker and I look at it and it looks so strange that I really don't want to eat it.

I ask what that is there on that plate and get told that it's pork. I've never eaten pork in my life. We have chops, baked dinners every Sunday and sausages and stews: that's the tucker that I like. I don't know this food and or where it comes from. It could've come all the way from China for all I know.

I know where the tucker I eat comes from. Sausages from the butcher's and chops from sheep that lives out in the paddock. When we can afford it, Mummy buys one from the farmers and the boys hang it on the verandah in the old house at Koora and cut it up. But I gotta admit it don't look good coming home from school and there's a dead sheep with no skin on its back, hanging from the rafters, dripping blood into a bucket. That sure ain't a pretty sight.

So I don't eat the pork. I don't like the look of that one. My father wants to make me happy; he tries so hard, ordering me a Coke and anything that I want. What I want is a hamburger but there's no hamburgers on the menu. I nibble bits and pieces and try to look happy but I'm not. I try so hard but he pours me a shandy and I don't drink stuff like that, only Coke. I think I'm angry with him because he doesn't know me. Anyway, Mummy would've went crook if I would have drunk it. I think I still resent him getting married and not coming home. When we're leaving, Cora asks me if I liked it. I tell her I would have preferred a hamburger better.

***

The Cherry Pickers is in rehearsals at the Mews Theatre Workshop in Sydney. Lynnie's playing a minor role. When Sir Robert Helpmann sees her, he wants Lynnie to be the first Aboriginal model, with her face plastered all over Australia and overseas, but just like me, she's a bush bunny. She couldn't leave her family for that long.

The Cherry Pickers play doesn't end up getting performed. My father closes it up. It's because there's this show on TV called *Boney* and they have an Indian man named Kamal acting as a Blackfella. In protest, my father shuts his own play down. All those family members who were going to act in it—Aunty June, Aunty Flora and Lynnie—are devastated but they understand why.

The school holidays are coming up. My Dad and Cora have a place up near Taree now and Mummy asked me, 'Do you wanna go and spend the holidays up there?' 'Yeah.' It's gonna be so great, I think. I go up and visit our Mob on the Purfleet Mission and I have a couple of friends there now so that's real good. My father tries his hardest to make it a good visit; he spoils me a lot, but it's a nightmare.

I go home to Mummy and my family, feeling bad that my visit wasn't a real good one for anyone. I know my Dad tried very hard to make me happy. I tell Mummy that he said to me, 'When you finish high school, if you want, you can go to university. You can be whatever you want to be and university would be good for you'. Mummy tells me to think about it—it's a good idea if that's what I want. I think about it for a minute. I know in my heart I'm a bush bunny; I couldn't leave my family and live in Sydney.

I'm in Fourth Form now and Mummy takes me to a specialist. He's supposed to be the best in Australia—he's from England. I gotta have my ankle operated on, the one that I hurt up in Sydney all those years ago. Mummy asks him to check out my back as well; I was born with a curvature of the spine and she just wants to make sure it's okay, too. He wants to operate on my back as well but Mummy won't let him.

The Tent Embassy

It's 1972 and the Aboriginal Tent Embassy is being set up in Canberra. Mummy knows my father's involved; he always lets her know what he's doing. Mummy's worried; she knows he's on bail and has bail conditions and that he's not allowed to leave the state, and Canberra's in another state. We sit glued to the TV hoping that we don't spot him; if the police did, he'd be back in jail.

We go over there one day to see him but we don't stay long. Mummy's worried Kevin and me will get hurt and then the Welfare will be involved. My father tries to protect us kids in his own way and tells her to watch out for us if any strangers come to town. He tells her to watch out for people—ones that wanna talk to us kids and ones with cameras.

He says they would be trying to get to him through us. I bet he's glad now that Mummy wouldn't let him take pictures of me and Kevin when he come home from jail. He knows Mummy don't need no telling. She's been doing that all our lives, protecting us while he was locked up. We watch it on TV, feeling proud that he's there trying to make changes for Blackfellas.

There's trouble at the Tent Embassy; the police are gonna come in and pull it down. This means that they'll arrest the ones there that are protesting. Mummy tells us to pray our father's not there, that they don't pick him up and send him back to jail. Kevin has to run up to the post office to use the public phone and get the switchboard to ring up people we know to find out if he's safe. Kevin comes home: yes, our father's safe!

I go into hospital and they get me ready for the operation on my ankle the next morning. Mummy's not here. I tell them, 'You gotta wait for Mummy. I can't go in there without her.' They wait awhile and tell me I gotta go into theatre. I start crying, then I look up and Mummy is there. She had to drive in from Koora, the whole twenty-seven miles, and there was roadworks on the way. I bet she was speeding for the first time in her life. She tells me she loves me and she'll be waiting for me. I tell her I love her, too. I'm so scared.

I have my leg operated on about two months before the Fourth Form School Certificate. I'm in hospital for a while and I gotta study for the exams while I'm here. They have a cage over my leg so that the blankets don't fall on the plaster which goes halfway up my leg. My brothers and sisters come to visit me and hide a packet of smokes down there when Mummy isn't looking.

***

Mummy doesn't know but I've been going out with a good-looking boy named John. He comes and visits me when she isn't around. It's time for me to come home from hospital and Mummy and Beryl come to pick me up. Mummy drives a Mini Minor now and I have to try to get in the back seat with my leg covered in plaster. Its pure murder, my leg is hurting so bad. We head home to Koora.

My leg isn't healing the way it's supposed to, though, so I gotta go back to hospital. I study for my exams which are getting closer and closer. I go home again and then go to school on crutches. I have a new nickname now in Koora: 'little Hutch with the three crutches'. (My last name is Hutchings).

At last, the crutches are gone but I have to wear boots to school to support my ankle. Beautiful white boots that come up to my knee, the kind that

Nancy Sinatra wears, like in the Elvis movie. Oh, I look so good and I feel so sexy. I reckon I've gotta be the coolest chick in school with my boots and my school uniform.

39

My mother's grave and the Gilbert name

I'm sixteen and Mummy is ready now to take me to my mother's grave in Parkes, with Aunty Doris. We're searching for her resting place. It's been a long time since anyone has been here. All we have is a plot number and a row number. These two women that I love have split up, walking each row, trying to pull from their memories where this grave would be, amongst the pain in their hearts.

They look for the plot number that the council man gave Mummy. She couldn't remember where the grave was after all these years. I follow behind them, looking and feeling helpless. Their tears are falling as they walk beside the other people's graves, looking for the grave number. All of a sudden Mummy sings out—she found it.

We all come together and stand in front of this little, tiny mound of dirt with nothing on it. Nothing. Not one flower or even a little white cross, nothing but dirt. These two wonderful old women that I love so dearly sit on each side of my mother's grave and try to straighten the dirt up, try hard to make it look nice. They sit sobbing, rubbing the top of the grave as if they are patting the back of a baby, making it feel better. I'm sure they are talking to my mother, to Goma, deep in their hearts, and I'm pretty sure that she's listening.

    I stand at the end of the grave, just watching them silently. I wanna cry 'cause they're crying and I can feel their pain deep down inside me but I wanna be strong for them, too. I know if I start, their tears and heartache will only get worse. That will break them in two; so I hold back and stay strong for them.

    I stand back a bit from the grave, not knowing what to do or say. I've been deliberately walking in Mummy's footprints because I didn't wanna be the one to find it. There is no sign that anybody has been here in sixteen years. Why haven't her other family remembered her enough to put a bunch of flowers on her grave?

I know exactly why we haven't been here before now. Mummy wouldn't have brought me here until she thought I could handle it. I can see on their faces the years of keeping the pain inside. Of not being able to cry, not only for my mother but for their little brother and their family. I see the thoughts of 'if only' flicker across their faces. *If only it never happened. If only they could have stopped it.*

They get up to leave the grave, leaving me there by myself. They cuddle me and tell me they love me. Mummy and Aunty Doris walk away, tears rolling down their cheeks. They are holding onto each other so tight, trying to hold each other up so they don't fall down into all their pain. I see their legs buckling but I see their strength, too, as they cling tight. I hear their sobbing and my heart is weeping, too, but there's nothing I can do to make it better for them. I feel their pain but I'm helpless.

I watch them, making sure they are back at the car, making sure they got there safe without either one of them fainting from the pain. I bend beside the top of my mother's grave and try to cry for this woman I've never known. I hurt deep down inside. I tell her I'm sorry I didn't know her and that she never got to be my mother and that I'm sorry she wasn't; but I've got Mummy and she'd be happy about that.

I take off my special necklace that Mummy brought me years ago and I dig a hole and bury it into her resting place. I tell her I love her and hope my necklace will keep her happy. She's got something of me now. I tell her Kevin is good and that he's a good big brother. He is not hurting so bad now and he knows it wasn't my fault she died. Me and him are pretty close now that we're grown-up.

We can finally talk about it now. I can ask Mummy little bits and pieces about my mother and father but I don't ask too much because I feel her pain stabbing her the moment she starts talking. I learn to pick my moment if I wanna talk about grown-up things with Mummy. It's best to get her while she's driving. I'm sure, this way, she's able to hide her pain and sorrow from me by looking straight ahead.

40

A daughter's love

I tell Mummy that I love her and how lucky I am that she decided to take us home. She says, 'No, Babe, it was Ned, too'. (Ned is Daddy's real name.) 'We kept you and Kevin because of him as well.' Mummy had told him she was worried about how they was gonna keep us all. It was already hard for them as a family; they had everyone else to take care of. Mummy knew it would be much harder with an extra two but Daddy said, 'We can't let these two little kids be split up'.

'June wanted to take you and Raymond wanted Kevin. We both wouldn't let you be split up. You had to stay together. That's what families do.'

I say a silent 'thank you' to Daddy. I don't and can't think of having any family other than the one I have. I thank Biamie[1] for giving me them.

Mummy tells me why she had to make us four younger ones State Wards. They couldn't afford all the kids, money was hard to come by. They didn't know when or where the work would be. She tells the story of how her and Aunty Doris would walk for miles to fell some trees, getting paid almost nothing—one shilling and threepence—so that they could buy food to feed both families. And that's all it bought; there was never any money for anything more.

I picture these two women walking for miles, leaving us younger kids with the older kids to look after us. Swinging an axe in the same way a man does with sweat dripping off them, muscles rippling in their arms as they work non-stop to earn that meagre money. I see them trudging their way home exhausted, the sun shining down on their backs, too tired to talk to each other, preserving their energy to go

---

[1] Biamie is our Creator, the great spiritual being.

home and then be mothers to a tribe of kids. I feel tears well up as I wish that maybe, if I hadn't been born, it would have been easier for them.

Mummy talks about when her own parents died. She was young, just seventeen, when the Welfare took my father and Aunty Flora away; and Mummy got them back and tried to raise them. How the paddocks was their only hope for work—picking cherries, oranges—anything that would provide food for everyone's mouth. How Aunty Doris tried to help keep the family together. How, without each other, they would've been lost. These two old women would never have coped without each other to help raise their families.

***

When Mummy and me go driving anywhere, I would often ask her about my grandparents, about what she used to do as a kid growing up in Condo and Three Ways. What had life been like for her and my father's generation?

After the years of silence or just hearing odd snippets, Mummy would now tell me great stories. Like how my father was the baby, how he was spoilt just like me and about what they all used to do in those times. How they used to ride the horses through the paddocks when they were picking the oranges. How they all looked after the animals out in the bush and how my father had a kangaroo for a pet but she can't remember its name now.

She tells me how him, Aunty June and Aunty Flora used to give the neighbours heaps by picking their fruit. She laughs as she tells each yarn but the pain and heartache crackles her voice as she remembers. She talks about her own mother, this wonderful and gentle woman who loved them all but was also tough on them, too. She talks about her Dad, a proud man, who loved his family and loved his wife. She tells me they sang a lot at their home. (Mummy sounds like Sharon when she sings, real soulful, just like the country and western stars that we used to listen to on the wireless.)

I gently swing the talk around now to us, me and Kevin. I say to her, 'Mummy, it must have been so hard for you all those times. Travelling doing the fruits with all us kids and outrunning the Welfare all the time.'

She tells me a secret. 'It was, Babe; and it wasn't just that, running away from the Welfare all the time, trying to make a living. We had to run as soon as anyone found out we were the Gilberts. As soon as they found out what happened in the family, they persecuted us. I was so scared for you kids. I had to get youse out of there so youse wouldn't be hurt no more. You all have been hurt enough as it was.'

I'm sitting and crying deep inside for this woman. This amazing Aboriginal woman who is my mother, who has only shown strength and dignity; strength to keep her kids and her brother's kids safe; to stop the world's cruelty towards four innocent children who did nothing, and who tried to protect her other kids from the poverty and the hurt as well.

The sound of gunfire

One day, me and Mummy are driving to Condo to see family when, at long last, Mummy talks about the night of the murder; not how it happened or why but what happened afterwards. My father turns up at her door crying in the middle of the night. It's January 1957 and I'm three months old. He tells Mummy, his sister, what he's done. He has the gun in his hand. She tells him he has three choices: to give her the gun; to hand himself in; or to go and turn the gun on himself.

My father gives her the gun. They get me and Kevin inside the house and then my father hands himself in to the police in Parkes.

Hearing this story at sixteen, it dawns on me. Mummy had probably seen my mother's body in the van where she had been shot dead. Mummy would have seen the blood that my one-and-a-half-year-old brother, Kevin, had seen. I cry for them both, and of course, for this man who is my father. I cry for Kevin and myself, surrounded or covered by the blood of our mother as she lay in the car with us.

Mummy blames herself. I can see it on her face. Her next words I hear loud and clear.

'If only I'd had enough beds to go around for everyone. But there was only enough as it was. If only they would have stayed that night...'

If only. If only. How do I tell her that it wasn't her fault? I can't because I know that nothing I could say would make a difference.

41

Motorbikes and life

In 1973, I get my School Certificate and I'm still in love with John. Even though Mummy has threatened to shoot him with the shotgun, he's still hanging around.

Mummy and me are heading to the opal fields to go opal mining. It's been a dream for both of us. The car is already packed when Mummy gets a phone call (yes, we've finally got the phone on!): Kevin's had a motorbike accident. They pulled him out from under a truck in Wagga. They thought they were gonna pull out a body, not a person. He's hurt bad.

Mummy's knees buckle as she takes the call. I stand beside her, waiting to catch her if she falls. I know something's wrong but I don't know what yet. She hangs the phone up, sobbing. She tells me it's Kevin. We get in the car and drive to Wagga. He's bad; he's in the hospital and has plaster all over his body but he's alive and that's the most important thing.

Back in Koora, I have a Kawasaki 100 that I normally fly around on. Mummy tells me I'm not allowed to have the bike anymore; I might have an accident and not be as lucky as Kevin. I don't argue. I seen the pain in her heart when she was on the phone and in the hospital but I figure that I'll wait for my chance to talk her out of that when we get home—I had no intention of giving up my bike. Anyway, I have no choice. When we come back from Wagga, she takes a hammer and goes and smashes my bike up, first the battery, then the bike. Tears roll down her cheeks as she does it.

And so life goes on for all of us. We still work in the paddocks. Our family has grown over the years and I have a lot more nieces and nephews. Lynnie has a little boy named Willie but he's more mine than hers, we share him. Kevin still lives with Maureen in Wagga 'cause Sam's in the army. Meryl drives the preschool bus for the Erambie Mission in Cowra.

42

Writing in Ghent, New York

It is 2006 and I'm sitting here, thousands of miles from home in Ghent, New York, at an Artist's Retreat called Art Omi. As I write, I'm thinking how my father must have felt in Grafton Jail when he saw his two children for the first time in seven years. I wonder how often he thought about us growing up, being kids, laughing in the sunshine or crying when we fell over and hurt ourselves. We was living in a world totally different to the one he was in—one surrounded by thick walls and metal bars.

Apart from the few visits in the fourteen-and-a-half years he spent in jail, my father only knew us through photographs. He only read about us in letters and had only seen us in real life three times. Mummy had always written to him all those years, telling him about us and sending him photographs, baby photos and school photos. I have these photos with me now. My heart breaks when I look at the picture of me and Kevin playing marbles with the other kids and I turn the photo over and read the words on the back. They are the same as what Mummy had written to Nanna and Pop.

Kerry (in front) and Kevin (2nd on right) playing marbles.

'To our Daddy with love, Love Kevin and Kerry xxxx'

Kerry, aged one: 'To my Daddy with love, Love Kerry xxx'

I imagine the letters that Mummy would have written to him in Long Bay and Grafton Jails, and Morisset Hospital.

> Dear Kevin,
> Just a quick note to say all is well. Kevin and Kerry are real good. Kerry is getting bigger now and so is Kevin; they are both good kids. They send you their love. All the family is well... We'll be heading to Orange to do the cherries in a couple of weeks. Hopefully, soon you'll be able to come home.
> Take care of yourself...
> God bless

>Your loving sister
>Joyce and family xxxxx
>P.S. Sending you photos of the kids

Mummy always says 'God bless' as you hang up the phone and I say it back to her, even though I don't believe in God. How could God have given my family the life that he had given them when they are good people and didn't deserve the hardship?

I ask myself: *How hard was it when all he would have wanted was to reach out and touch us, to cuddle us? How hard was it for him knowing that a wall with iron bars stopped him from touching, from loving his children? How must he have felt when he watched us walk away from him, not knowing when he would see us again?*

He knew that we was fruit pickers 'cause he was one, too. He knew that money was hard to come by.

He would've known that, sometimes, Mummy went without tucker to feed her kids, his kids. He would have understood that we couldn't see him a real lot. He would have been happy that we were with Mummy, that the Welfare never got us or that me and Kevin weren't separated from each other. *When he saw us in jail, did he hope or think that, one day, he might be able to hold us as a father? That he'd be able to pick his little girl and his son up and feel their arms around him?*

How did he cope deep down in his heart, fearing that he might never get outta jail 'cause he was sentenced to life for the murder of our mother? Did he know that, by the time he was released, we would no longer be children but teenagers?

How much did his heart break when he knew he still told a lie about my mother and me when they made that show on television thirteen years later?

In his book *Living Black,* my father writes his memory of seeing me, aged seven, and Kevin, and how he felt seeing his daughter who looked like him.

***

I sit and think of Mummy. How hard it was for her: so many hungry kids; always working, making sure we always had a feed. She could make good tucker from just a bit of mince, a potato and an onion. I wonder now how many meals she went without, making sure that her kids were fed. No. I don't wonder, I know. Memories come back to me of sitting at the kitchen table on the Island and she doesn't sit down with us. She tells us she has already eaten. No thought was in my child's mind that she was going without.

How must she have cried to herself so many times? How often did she feel responsible for the heartache that was in the family? Feeling that, somehow, if she could have done more, maybe she could have prevented what life dished out to us. I know she always felt responsible for the things she had no control of. Would she have whispered the words to her own mother that she didn't mean to let her down? She tried hard to keep her promise to keep the family together. In her whispers to her, did she tell her she did the best she could?

I see Mummy so clearly as I read my father's words. I have seen her that way every time we walked into a paddock, a dirty, dusty paddock. Every time we had to climb a ladder or sling it over our shoulders to carry it to the next tree, I see her. The sweat dripping off her, an old torn hat on her head, a man's flannelette shirt on, trying to protect her skin. I see her and I see me and each and every member of my family right down to my own children because that's where we come from, the paddocks. That has been our life. I'm a fruit picker by trade. I say those words with pride in my heart because that is who I am, that is my family. I am Joyce's girl, the cherry picker's daughter.

The End

www.ingramcontent.com/pod-product-compliance
Lightning Source LLC
Chambersburg PA
CBHW050552170426
43201CB00011B/1671